MW01298710

No matter how big any challenge is,
don't give up!

THERE IS HOPE

I was healed from metastatic kidney cancer through faith in Jesus

Gregory M Doublas, MBA

authorHOUSE®

AuthorHouse™
1663 Liberty Drive
Bloomington, IN 47403
www.authorhouse.com
Phone: 1 (800) 839-8640

We maybe contacted at Gospeltruth@frontier.com

Published by AuthorHouse 04/10/2018

ISBN: 978-1-5462-2794-6 (sc)
ISBN: 978-1-5462-2819-6 (e)

Library of Congress Control Number: 2018901540

Print information available on the last page.

To the glory of my Lord Jesus, the
Holy Son of the Living God.

Contents

Introduction

Very often we face difficulties in this life that appear to be like great mountains, impossible to overcome. I also faced a great mountain I couldn't conquer on my own. I was diagnosed with kidney cancer, and shortly afterward, the doctor removed my left kidney. Unfortunately this cancer proved to be very dangerous and had spread to my lungs, and it became what they called a *metastatic cancer*. As a result, the doctor gave me a death sentence, but the Lord Jesus had something different for me, a life sentence.

Not only did the Lord heal me by removing the cancerous nodules from my lungs, but while I was going through these difficult times, He gave me *peace* in my heart and *hope* through His Word that everything would be all right.

And so I want to encourage you to remember there is *hope*, no matter how difficult the situation may be that you are going through in your life right now, have *faith* in the Lord Jesus, *trust* and *believe* in Him, and He will provide a *new way* for you where there may appear there is none. Scripture teaches us, "With God all things are possible" (Matt. 19:26).

Don't give up. There is hope.

Faith in God Brings Miracles

What Is Faith?

In his epistle to Hebrews, the apostle Paul wrote, "Now faith is the substance of things hoped for, the evidence of things not seen" (Heb. 11:1). Accordingly, faith is to expect to receive through prayer the things you *don't see* and those things you don't have.

But in order to receive from God something we have asked for in prayer, we must have faith in Him. Without faith, Scripture teaches us, it is impossible to receive anything. The apostle Paul wrote, "But without faith it is impossible to please Him: for he that cometh to God must believe that *He is,* and that He is a *Rewarder* of them that *diligently* seek Him" (Heb. 11:6).

So then we need to believe two things when we come before God in prayer:

1. That He is who He says He is, the Almighty God.
2. And that He rewards (provides) those who seek Him diligently, that is, those who believe and seek Him persistently with all their heart.

Abraham's Faith

There is a lot for all of us to learn about faith from the faith Abraham had toward God. Abraham was a hundred years old and without a son to inherit the blessings the Lord God had promised him, but yet he trusted God when He told him that despite his old age, he would have a son. Genesis 15:1–6 says, "After these things the word of the Lord came unto Abram in a vision, saying, fear not, Abram: I am thy shield, and thy exceeding great reward."

Scripture teaches us that God is unchangeable: "Jesus Christ the same yesterday, and today, and forever" (Hebrews 13:8). Since He is the same today, He is able to reward us today also if we believe in Him as did Abraham. In Genesis 15:2 we read again, "And Abram said, Lord God, what wilt thou give me, seeing I go childless, and the steward of my house is this Eliezer of Damascus?"

You see, the only successor Abraham had was a servant, but God responded to him with hope, "And, behold, the word of the Lord came unto him, saying, this shall *not* be thine heir; but he that shall come forth out of thine own bowels shall be thine heir" (Genesis 15:4).

Further we read, "And He brought him forth abroad, and said, look now toward heaven, and tell the stars, if thou be able to number them: and He said unto him, so shall thy seed be. And Abraham *believed* in the Lord; and he counted it to him for righteousness" (Genesis 15:5–6). And because he *believed* in God, not only did he obtain a promise from the Lord to have an heir, but he also received the gift of *righteousness*, that is, Abraham was declared to be virtuous before God, because of his trust in Him.

Further Scripture teaches us that Abraham believed in *hope* where there was no hope, as we read in the New Testament, in Romans 4:18–22 where it says, "Who against hope believed in hope, that he might become the father of many nations; according to that which was spoken, so shall thy seed be. And being not weak in faith, he considered not his own body now dead, when he was about an hundred years old, neither yet the deadness of Sarah's womb." And Sarah was ninety years old!

Abraham believed he would have a child even though it seemed impossible, humanly speaking. We also need to believe in God's Word rather than the impossible situations that may be against us, because believing in God always brings miracles. When we believe He is able to perform what He has promised, then all things become possible. Nothing is too hard or too great for God as it says in Jeremiah 32:27, "Behold, I am the Lord, the God of all flesh: is there anything too hard for me?"

We can overcome any challenge we face in life by believing the Lord is able to provide a way, no matter how difficult or challenging a situation is. Nothing is too great for the Almighty God.

David's Faith

Here is another example of great faith. Rather than fear, David went with courage and determination to face Goliath. He didn't consider the odds against him, and he didn't think of what was obvious—that it was impossible for him to defeat the giant. Instead he believed in the Lord God and the supernatural. He believed the Lord God would help him do what was impossible to do by himself.

We read in 1 Samuel 17:45–48, "Then said David to the Philistine, thou comest to me with a sword, and with a spear, and with a shield, but I come to thee in the *name* of the Lord of hosts, the God of the armies of Israel, whom thou hast defied."

Do you see what David did? He *invoked* the name of the Lord God and *trusted* in Him. David was making sure every demon knew he was coming against Goliath armed *only* with the supernatural power of God Almighty. And in the following verse, we read where David proclaimed the victory he would obtain through God before he even had it. That is, he *believed* and *acted* with faith and certainty that he would receive the things that were *unseen*. That's why he said, "This day will the Lord deliver thee into mine hand; and I will smite thee, and take thine head from thee; and I will give the carcasses of the host of the Philistines this day unto the fowls of the air, and to the wild beasts of the earth; that all the earth may know that there is a God in Israel" (1 Sam. 17:46). Now, that's Godly courage that brings victory through faith even against the most impossible of situations.

David also made sure to give God the glory by declaring so that the world would know that God is the one who fights for him. "And all this assembly shall know that the Lord saveth not with sword and spear: *for the battle is the Lord's*, and He will give you into our hands" (1 Sam. 17:47).

We also need to recognize that as believers in Christ, the battles we face daily in our lives are not ours to fight, but the Lord's as we read also in 2 Chronicles 20:15, "*for the battle is not yours, but God's.*" That's what the Almighty God said to King Jehoshaphat of Judah, a man who trusted in the God of Abraham, Isaac and Jacob. He asked God's help, when one day an army that was far greater that the army of Judah, came against him. God heard Jehoshaphat's prayer and destroyed the enemy by causing such confusion amongst the enemy soldiers, that they began killing each other, and without Judah having to fight, the enemy was completely destroyed (2 Chronicles 20:24).

Like David, we need to meet all challenges with *godly courage* and be fully convinced the Lord is with us, as He was with David who *ran* toward the army to meet the Philistine as we read in 1 Samuel 17:48.

You may be going through a tough challenge right now, but have faith and trust in the Lord Jesus. He has the answer to all things. Believe that He is *able* to deliver you from the challenge you are facing. Believe, no matter how impossible it may seem to you, or to those around you, because with Jesus, you will be able to overcome the problem no matter how big it is that you are facing.

The Lord can provide a way for you, as He did for me when a CT scan showed I had many nodules in my lungs as a result of kidney cancer. Also later, after the initial discovery, the doctor had told me during the follow-up appointment two months later, that the nodules had multiplied.

Despite the devastating news, the Lord gave me the strength to say in front of the doctor, "The Lord will provide a *way* for me, just as He provided a way to the Israelites when they were facing the Red Sea and Pharaoh's army approaching from behind."

Because I believed in Him, the Lord Jesus provided a way for me also by removing the nodules from my lungs when the doctor had given me no hope, and that's because with the Lord all things are possible. And He can do the same for you as well, whether you are dealing with an incurable illness, a job loss, a failing business, an addiction, a family situation, a financial problem, or the devastating illness of the mind, depression, and so on. No matter what it may be, know that the Lord Jesus can deliver you from any problem by providing a *new way* for you. *Trust* in Him and *believe* He is able to do what He has promised in His Word.

To Jairus, a Jewish ruler of the synagogue whose daughter had died, Jesus said, "Be not afraid, only believe" (Mark 5:36). And because Jairus *believed*, his daughter was raised from the dead.

We also need to remember what the Lord Jesus said, "That men ought *always* to pray" (Luke 18:1–8). That means, we must never lose our hope, but to *trust* in Him always and continue in prayer.

Do not stop praying, and if you don't get an answer right away, it doesn't mean He didn't hear you or that He doesn't want to answer you. Rather it means you need to learn to *trust* in Him and continue to believe He has something better for you. Be assured that He knows all about the challenge you are facing. Don't lose your hope.

You see, He always provides an answer. If you didn't get what you have asked of Him as quick as you might have expected, it doesn't mean He didn't answer you. If He didn't say anything, then His *silence* is your answer. He wants you to learn to *trust* in Him. Therefore, always persevere and in due time, He will bring what you have asked of Him, and His timing always turns out to be the best for us and for His glory.

Through the following verses, the Lord gave us an example that illustrates how He, Himself will deal with us if we *persist* in our supplications and don't give up.

Luke 18:2–7 we read, "There was in a city a judge, which feared not God, neither regarded man. And there was a widow in that city; and she came unto him, saying, avenge me of mine adversary. And he would not for a while: but afterward he said within himself, though I fear not God, nor regard man, yet because this widow troubleth me, I will avenge her, lest by her continual coming she weary me. And the Lord said, hear what the unjust judge saith. And shall not God avenge His own elect, which cry day and night unto Him, though He bear long with them? I tell you that He will avenge them speedily."

By His Word, He is instructing us to be *persistent* and not give up. We are to keep praying and to be *expecting* with *faith* to receive from Him.

If you persist, He will provide a *new way* for you out of any challenge that you are facing right now. He will bring you a miracle, just as He did for me. Don't give up.

My Testimony

We Are Temporary

In his first epistle, the apostle Peter wrote, "For all flesh *is* as grass, and all the glory of man as the flower of grass. The grass withereth, and the flower thereof falleth away" (1 Peter 1:24). Through this verse, Scripture is teaching us that we are temporary in this life, and quite often, no matter how well we maintain our bodies, eat the right foods, exercise, and do all the other good things, our bodies still may break down, and that's because we are temporary.

When something goes wrong, we often don't have any pain, discomfort, or signs to indicate that something bad has happened. Yet we may go to the doctor for a routine checkup for cholesterol or other things we do on a routine basis, and there we find out that something's terribly wrong.

In the book of Genesis, we read the story of when Joseph brought his father, Jacob, to introduce him to Pharaoh after Jacob and his family had come to Egypt to avoid the famine that was in the land of Canaan:

> "And Pharaoh said unto Jacob, how old are you?" And Jacob said unto Pharaoh, "The days of the years of my *pilgrimage* are an hundred and thirty years; few and evil have the years of my life been, and have

> not attained unto the days of the years of the life of my fathers in the days of their pilgrimage" (Gen. 47:8–9).

Well, that's how it is. This life is temporary, it's like a pilgrimage. We are not here forever. And our bodies are temporary, as we read above in the first epistle of Peter, and as such, they are subject to failure.

And so it was the case with me when I discovered a problem with my body when sometime during the spring of 2015, I began to have a dry cough that wouldn't stop. At night I wouldn't cough, but during the day, it would go on and on. Often I would be talking to somebody, and the cough would start. It was disrupting and embarrassing.

This continued for months, and finally my wife said, "You need to go to the doctor."

Well, I didn't think I needed to go because I never had any health problems all my life. By the grace of God, I never even knew what pain was, like a headache, toothache, or earache. I was always healthy. I went to the doctor for routine checkups, like a blood test for cholesterol and other predictable things. So I thought I didn't need to go to the doctor just for the cough. It would *go away*, I thought.

Well, it didn't go away. It continued on and on. Finally my wife convinced me to see the doctor. And so in the middle of August 2015, I went to the doctor and explained the problem, and he suggested some over the-counter medication, like cough syrup. I did that for a few days, but nothing changed. I went back and had X-rays done, which showed nothing wrong in my lungs or chest, but the cough continued on. So I went back to my doctor and asked to see a pulmonologist.

And so, in the beginning of September, I visited a pulmonologist, who took me through some tests. The first day, I had this computer testing where I blew through it at various stages to determine the strength of the lungs and see if there were any blockages. After I finished, they asked me to have a seat until I was to see the doctor.

But as we go through this life, during good and bad times, God is always in charge and has a purpose for everything. No matter what we go through, He knows about it because He is the Almighty God, and in His hands all things exist. He knows about the smallest details and the large things we encounter in life. He knows everything.

Witnessing for Christ

During this time when I was very concerned about this cough, God had something different in His mind. As I was waiting in the lobby for the nurse to call me to see the pulmonologist, I was watching the news on my cell phone and waiting patiently. I noticed the time went by, like an hour and a half, and everybody who had been there in the waiting room was gone, even someone who had come after me. And so I got up and went to the front desk and said, "I think you forgot about me."

"Oh, honey, I'm so sorry. Have a seat, and I'll call you right away" said the lady at the front desk. Well, she came back within minutes and said, "The lady who did the computer testing for you failed to give me your file, and I didn't know that you were waiting here." And so, right away she took me into an exam room to wait for the doctor. As I look back about it, this delay was not accidental.

Within a few minutes, a young man wearing a white jacket came in, and he introduced himself, saying he was a medical student working with this doctor in the field of pulmonology. He began to do a physical examination of me, and made a lot of notes. He asked me to do various things, like hold my hand straight as he was pressing down on it. I sat on the table, and then he was pressing on my legs to determine the level of my strength. He also checked for pain in my lymph nodes and elsewhere.

I detected he had an accent and at one point, I felt *these words come out from deep inside of me*, and I said to him, "Many years ago, I came from Greece. Where did you come from?"

"My father was from Turkey, and later he had moved to Iraq" he said.

I asked, "Oh, are you a Turk or an Iraqi?"

No he said, "We're called Turkmen."

"Well, I have heard about your nationality" I responded.

As he continued with the physical examination, he said a little later, "Mr. Doublas, you're a very strong man."

Immediately I said, "The Lord is my strength." And right away I continued, "Do you know the Lord?"

As he was writing down notes, he stopped momentarily and pointed his fingers upward, "Yes, God" he said.

Then I said, "The Lord Jesus is the Lord, and He's the *only* way to heaven. There's no other way for any of us to go to heaven except *through* Him."

He stopped writing, looked at me and said, "Well, did you pray for this?" He meant my cough, because he knew of-course why I was there.

"Yes, I prayed" I responded.

He returned, "What did He tell you?" And by that I believed he meant, "What did this Jesus tell you about your cough?"

I said, "He didn't tell me anything." And of course that was the truth, because I have been praying, but the Lord had not provided an answer. As I know now, it was not the right time yet.

Then he replied, "Then what's the purpose?"

And right then, the instant he finished talking, I heard a very clear voice to my right side that said, "This is the purpose." It was the Lord. I knew it, because when God speaks two things become very clear: You know deep inside who spoke, and second, you know unmistakably what He said.

You see, the purpose of all this, as I found out later, was for this man to hear the message of the gospel, that Jesus is the only way to heaven. I didn't ask what his beliefs were nor did I talk negatively about anything that might pertain to religion. No doubt, this whole conversation was directed by the Lord. God wants us to witness to other people about His Son Jesus, and if we're willing, He will grant us an opportunity even when we don't expect it, to bring the good news of the kingdom of Heaven to someone.

I am convinced that the Lord has set a time for certain people to hear the message of the gospel in a personal way, because this has happened with me many times in the past, where I have witnessed to people of other faiths. According to my experience, this can happen when He chooses the time and the person to hear about His Holy Son Jesus.

God expects us to be *willing* to testify for Him; otherwise He will not force us into anything by overriding our free will that He has granted to us.

Most days in the morning, I would say, "Lord, I'm willing to talk to somebody about you. Who would you want me to witness to today?" And I believe, when we do that He will present an opportunity to witness to people. And that's what happened to me that day. I don't know what this man did with the words he heard from me that day, that's between him and God only, but I do know beyond any doubt, it was a divine appointment for us to meet.

As believers in Christ, we ought to be aware of the importance of witnessing, or *confessing* for Jesus. That is, telling other people about Him without shame or fear. The apostle Paul wrote about the significance of confessing by saying, "That if thou shalt confess with thy mouth the Lord Jesus, and shalt believe in thine *heart* that God hath raised him from the dead, thou shalt be saved. For with the heart man believeth unto righteousness; and with the *mouth* confession is made unto salvation" (Rom. 10:9–10). You see, witnessing or confessing Jesus to other people is not only that we convey the saving message of the Gospel to people, but it's also important for our own salvation.

On the other hand, if we are ashamed or fearful of what people would say about us if we talk about Jesus or witness the truth of the gospel, the Lord said He also would be ashamed of us before His Father in heaven as we read, "Whosoever therefore shall be ashamed of me and of my words in this adulterous and sinful generation; of him also

shall the Son of Man be ashamed, when He cometh in the glory of His Father with the holy angels" (Mark 8:38).

And it would be a terrible thing to be found rejected by God on that dreadful day of judgement.

And so, I did go back for a second visit to the pulmonologist, but I discovered soon that the medication he gave me was not doing anything to help me. It was making no difference whatsoever. So I didn't go back; nor did I finish the medication. And I have concluded that my cough was not the only purpose I went to see this doctor.

I was there because of a divine appointment that only the Almighty God could have made possible. He works in mysterious ways. And I believe, if we are willing to do His work, He has an appointed time that we may be a shining light for the Lord, by witnessing to somebody. And these God given appointments, could be during good or bad times in our life.

Jesus told his disciples, "I am the way, the truth, and the life. *No man comes to the Father but by me*" (John 14:6). And that is what I told this man at the pulmonologist's office, that Jesus is the only way. It's a significant truth for all people, all over the world to know, that there is no other name that we may call upon to provide a way to heaven for us. Nor is there any other person or name, in heaven or on earth, to call upon to seek help during difficult, challenging times, like the kind I went through, except the name of Jesus.

It was through the name of Jesus that the apostles Peter and John healed a man who was born "impotent" from his mother's womb. This man had never walked. And one day, as Peter and John were going to the temple, this man was sitting there at the gate of the temple, asking people to give him some money. And Peter said, "Silver and gold I have none, but what I have I'll give to you for free. In the name of Jesus Christ of Nazareth, stand up and walk" (Acts 3:6).

Immediately the man stood and walked. In fact, the Bible says he was *leaping* for joy, but when the Jews saw this man walking, they were utterly amazed at Peter and John, thinking they were the ones who had healed this man. But Peter was quick to direct all the glory to Jesus saying, "And His name through faith in His name hath made this man strong, whom ye see and know: yea, the faith which is by Him (Jesus) hath given him this perfect soundness in the presence of you all" (Acts 3:16).

As a result of this miracle, Peter was given an opportunity to witness to the leaders of the Jewish people by declaring to them with godly courage, "Neither is there salvation in any other: for there is none other name under heaven given among men, whereby we must be saved" (Acts 4:12).

And this is an example for all of us to follow. We must imitate Peter and the other apostles of the Lord, who with boldness and without shame and fear, proclaimed that Jesus is the *only* way, because God the Father made Him to be Lord over all things and of all people, by giving Him all *authority* in heaven and on earth according to Matthew 28:18.

My cough continued, and toward the end of September, I decided to go back to my personal doctor. He suggested I have a blood test, so they made an appointment for me. The blood test came back, and they called from the doctor's office and said the doctor was not comfortable with something.

They didn't say exactly what it was, but the doctor wanted me to have another blood test.

And so I did go back a second time within a day and had another blood test and later I called to find out about the results, and the nurse told me that the doctor wanted to see me.

During this visit, the doctor told me that there were some things in the chemistry of my blood that he wasn't quite able to explain. Now I'm not sure if he didn't know what it was, or if he didn't want to tell me that something was wrong with me.

He said, "A hematologist knows more about the chemistry of the blood. We will make an appointment for you to see one."

Indeed, they made an appointment for me to see this hematologist at the local hospital, and around the middle of October, I went. After he saw the results of the blood tests I had with my personal doctor, he suggested a number of additional blood tests, like nine of them. He also sent me to get X-rays of nearly every part of my body because he thought, as he told me, I might have bone cancer. But he also was concerned about the possibility of liver disease, such as hepatitis.

I did all of those tests that the hematologist had recommended, and I went back to see him. He said he still wasn't sure exactly what it was, but he mentioned that the X-rays showed that there was no evidence of bone cancer. He was still concerned about liver disease. Again he mentioned hepatitis might be the problem.

I began to worry that there was something seriously wrong with me. He said he wanted to send me to another doctor, an internist across town at a different hospital. So they made an appointment for me.

In the middle of November, I saw the internist. After consulting the blood tests I'd had, he recommended an endoscopy. I did that toward the latter part of November 2015, and it came out okay. Then he suggested I have an ultrasound of my liver because he was concerned something was wrong in that organ.

So toward the end of November. I had an ultrasound. After I finished, he called me and said, something was there in the liver, a few spots. He couldn't tell however, exactly what the nature of those spots was, just that there was something there that showed up in the ultrasound. So he suggested I have an MRI of my liver.

Sometime at the beginning of December 2015, I had the MRI. I got ready to get into this tube and they gave me ear plugs because of the noise, also, they told me I would be in there thirty to thirty-five minutes. I complained about it, and I told the nurse, "Boy, I wish they'd told me that before. If I knew that this was so noisy and it takes so long, I may not have come." To be honest, when I looked at this big machine I thought, what would happen if it breaks down while I am in there, how would I get out? It may sound foolish, but I even thought about how would I get out of there if it catches on fire? I started thinking about a plan in case that happened.

But the nurse must have seen I was a "little" skeptical and said, "You'll be fine. It's for your own good. You need to take the test."

While the machine was running, I complained a couple of times, asking "how long yet would I have to be in here", but the nurse kindly told me, "Mr. Doublas, this is for your own good. Just a little bit longer and we're done." I know now that most likely, she was seeing things in there that through her experience knew they were not normal.

And she was right. This was good for me because, little did I know, through this noisy machine would we discover the real problem with my health.

After the MRI test ended, I went home, and within an hour the internist called me and said, "Mr. Doublas, I received the MRI test results rather quickly from the doctor who examined them. At this time, there appears nothing really is wrong with your liver. The spots appear to be on the benign side. But there's another problem. The MRI found that your left kidney has a large tumor on it. You need to call an urologist as soon as possible. Do you have an urologist?"

I did have an urologist that I had known for some time. I called his office and left a message with the reason for my call. To my surprise, the urologist called me back within about half hour, because now, of course, they have the convenience of seeing the results of tests through the computer immediately, anywhere they may be.

So he called me back and said, "Greg, we have a problem."

I asked, "What is it?"

He said, "Your left kidney has a large tumor, and it's cancerous."

That really surprised me. I felt like a brick had hit me on the face. I said, "Now wait a minute. How can you say it's cancerous when we didn't have a biopsy to prove that?"

He said, “I’m ninety-seven … no … ninety-nine percent sure it is cancerous, and I know this because of my experience.” and he continued, “But I can help you.”

“Oh, how can you help me?” I asked.

“I will take it out. During the past three years, the technology has improved enormously in this field.”

That really went the wrong way for me. I wasn’t ready to accept that I would lose a part of my body. I thought deep within myself but didn’t say out loud to him, *It’s easy for you to say you’ll remove my kidney, but for me, I’m not sure if I’m ready to part ways with a very important part of my body!*

I said to him, “Oh, I don’t know about this.”

He said, “No, Greg. We have to do this surgery. We have to take this kidney out. I’m going to make the arrangements for your surgery as soon as possible. The nurse will call you back with the day, the time, everything. So we’ll be in touch.”

And so that was that.

Now I don’t know if you have ever had any such thing happen to you, where you receive bad news or the doctor says to you, “Your left kidney has a large tumor, and it’s cancerous.” This type of news is very difficult to accept. He could have beaten around the bush or told me more tactfully that I had a tumor on my kidney, but I would rather have the truth. But you see, the truth sometimes is difficult to accept.

Nevertheless I had to go through this difficult time. As I said before, I had never had anything wrong with my body. Never. But then all of a sudden, I had what seemed to be a very serious problem. I never experienced any discomfort, pain, or anything to indicate there was something so wrong with me. But again, as I said before, we are temporary. No matter how well we take care of ourselves, our bodies may break down.

You know, in all the years of my life, I never been a smoker nor did I drink alcohol. I seldom had any fast food. I don't drink Pepsi or Coca-Cola or any of what you call "pop" drinks. I don't eat boxed food. I only eat what we cook at home, and I drink only water. Yet I had this issue with my kidney.

As we read earlier, the Lord spoke through the apostle Peter to tell us, "For all flesh *is* as grass, and all the glory of man, as the flower of grass. The grass withereth, and the flower thereof falleth away" (1 Peter 1:24). We are temporary, and our bodies do break down, no matter how well we take care of them, that's the nature we have in this life. Because we are temporary and our bodies are subject to breakdown, that leads me to the next issue that we all need to be aware of.

We don't know the time when we may pass on from this life. What is important is that we all need to be aware of that possibility, and be ready at any time to go from this life in a way that our life here would please God, and through faith in the Lord Jesus we may find eternal life in heaven. It is important that we be *ready* for that moment, because we just don't know when that may come.

As the urologist had told me, the nurse did call me and said, "The doctor would like you to go have a CT scan of your chest, abdomen, and pelvis to make sure there's nothing else wrong with you before the surgery. So I'm going to schedule for you to go and have these tests. After we have the results, I will call you. For now, we have scheduled your surgery to remove your kidney for January 12, 2016. You have to be here at five thirty in the morning."

Then she gave me the information of where to go to have the CT scans, and she told me again that she would talk to me as soon as they had the results of these scans.

On December 8, 2015, I went and had the CT scan of my chest, abdomen, and pelvis.

The next day, the nurse called me back and said, "Greg, I'm so sorry. I have bad news for you. I know you had an issue with your liver, and the cancer in your left kidney. But now I have more bad news. Your lungs appear to have multiple nodules. The doctor wants to see you as soon as possible. So I'm going to call you back after I arrange a date for you to see the doctor."

Have you ever had so many devastating news about your health in your life? I don't know how to explain accurately or adequately how it feels to hear all these bad news in such a very short time. When the nurse finished speaking, it felt like something very, very large hit me. It was not something that was physical, no, it was something that was dark, evil, and I felt it. I don't know how to explain it any better. And it was overwhelming.

And in the midst of this difficult time, right there when I was overwhelmed, confused and in fear, it felt like I had reached the depths of despair, and I was beginning to get into: *Why me? Why now?*

I was about to enter and stay in this vicious cycle of questioning all this about my health, but before I went too far with it, I heard a clear, soft voice saying, "I know about your situation." It was calm and reassuring, and I *knew* beyond any doubt, it was the Lord. He voice was what I needed most during this difficult time. He had come at the right time, as He always does.

Additionally, my mind was instantly directed, not by me, to Psalm 112: 1 where it says, "Blessed *is* the man who fears the Lord, who delights greatly in His commandments." And further in Psalm 112:7 where it says, "He shall not be afraid of evil tidings; his heart is fixed, trusting in the Lord."

"He" in verse 7 above, is the man who fears God, and evil tidings are bad news. As a result of what the voice of the Lord said to me, and through the words from His Holy Bible, this peace came upon me that I couldn't explain, and I was okay or "at peace" with what I heard about my health, and this cycle of, "*Why me? Why now?*" Stopped, thank God.

Without the Lord, I don't know how I could have manage to go on that day or the days that followed, but with God we can overcome any difficult time, even the worst of bad news.

Does God Talk?

I know many of my fellow Christians who are very skeptical, to say the least, when they hear someone say, "God spoke." But I have a question to all those who may indeed feel that way: Do you believe we serve a living or a dead God? If God is dead, let us all be merry and have a good time in this life, for there will be nothing else beyond that, no future for any of us!

But that's not the case. The creator of all things, the Almighty God, is alive and on His mighty throne, and He is in control of everything in heaven and on earth. Nothing happens by luck or chance anywhere or to anyone. And because He is Alive, through faith in Jesus, His Holy Son, truly there is a future.

Furthermore, in the Christian Churches, every year, at twelve midnight on the Saturday of the Holy Week, and for forty days thereafter (as it is in the Orthodox church), we chant, "Christ is risen from the dead." Well, I would ask then all those who are skeptical, who question whether God speaks—whether God does talk to people, what goes through your mind when you chant that hymn (Christ is risen from the dead)? That these words are simply part of a religious tradition?

The Lord Jesus is alive at all times, and as any other *living* person, He hears, He can see, and He does *talk*. In fact, He tries to talk to every one of us, but the worries of this life and the noise that exists all around us in these modern times, and the unbelief that exists among people, do not allow them to hear His voice. And so people come to the wrong conclusion that God is not alive, or they think, "He may have talked back then, thousands of years ago, but not now". And that is very wrong to think of the Creator of all things, the One who has in His hands the existence of the entire universe. The truth is He is well and alive.

For many people, when they encounter a devastating challenge, a truly difficult time that has befallen them where they come to the point to realize no-one else can help in this life, it is then that they may begin to think, "Well maybe He is alive." It is *most likely* during a difficult time again, that they may reconsider to change their attitude towards Him, and even come to believe in Him, and may take even the time to stand still and listen to Him talk. And that's because they happen to be in a bad spot, out of necessity. But it should not be this way. We should at all times, good or bad, *believe* in Him and give Him the honor that's due to Him as the Living God who also talks, and *thank* Him and *praise* Him for all the good things we enjoy every day from Him.

But there is another element to this issue of hearing from God. First, we need to get to *know* Him so that we may be able to *recognize* His voice. If we don't know Him personally, we will not recognize His voice either. Just like when someone calls us we don't know, we don't recognize his voice.

In the first book of Samuel, we read where, as a young child Samuel who had spent all his life up to that point serving in the temple of God, did not recognize the voice of the Lord, when God called him one night. Instead Samuel thought Eli the priest had called him as we read, "And the Lord called yet again, Samuel. And Samuel arose and went to Eli, and said, here am I; for thou didst call me. And he answered, I called not, my son; lie down again. Now Samuel *did not yet know* the Lord, neither was the word of the Lord yet revealed unto him" (1 Sam. 3:6–7).

And how do we get to know Him in order to recognize His voice when He speaks? By making a willing effort to *study* His Word (the Bible) unfailingly, by *believing* in Him, and by spending time in *prayer*.

We can see the importance of knowing God by reading the words spoken by a truly godly man, king David of Israel, who towards the end of his life, spoke to his son Solomon saying, "And thou, Solomon my son, *know* thou the God of thy father, and serve Him with a perfect heart and with a willing mind: for the Lord searcheth all hearts, and understandeth all the imaginations of the thoughts: if thou *seek* Him, He will be found of thee; but if thou forsake Him, He will cast thee off forever" (1 Chronicles 28:9).

Point to remember: If we seek God, we will find Him and we will know Him also, and as we pointed earlier in this book, God is the same, yesterday, today and forever.

I also have a personal experience that I would like to share with you on this same subject. When I came from Greece many years ago to attend higher education, the person responsible for the dorms where I was attending put me in the same room with a student from Kuwait. At that time, I didn't know the Lord as I do now. As a result, I didn't recognize His voice either.

Every night close to bedtime, I would see this man from Kuwait unfold this small rag in the middle of the two beds, kneel on it, and begin to pray. Night after night, he kept doing the same thing, and I sitting on my bed, kept watching him in amazement. He is so dedicated I thought.

One night as I was observing him, I heard a small, gentle and real voice on my right ear that said, "Do you see him? Why don't you pray also?"

I didn't know who spoke to me, but I accepted without questioning what the voice had said to me, and I felt truly embarrassed. I thought, *here is someone who is not a Christian, and he is praying so persistently and I am not.* And so, I began kneeling on my bed from then on, reciting the Lord's Prayer, the prayer I knew since I was a child. It was many years later when I thought again about that moment, and I knew without doubt that it was the Lord who spoke that night, and had moved me to begin praying.

You see, God does indeed talk, but again, if we don't know Him, we will certainly not know His voice either. But once we get to know Him, by developing a relationship with Him, we will know His voice as well. God wants a relationship with us, and not simply to know who He is like we know so many people we see on TV for example, but we really don't know them. He wants us to have even a closer relationship with Him, than the one we have with our earthly parents.

About His Word. The Bible is the Living Word of God, and when we study it with the same zeal we seek food for our bodies, a miracle takes place. Our faith in Him begins to grow.

In his epistle to the Romans, the apostle Paul wrote, "So then faith cometh by hearing, and hearing by the word of God." (Romans 10:17). So then faith is the result of studying the Bible, God's Word with zeal.

When we study His Word, Jesus comes in us and it is through Him then that our faith in Him rises, because He is the Living Word of God, that's His other name. In Revelation 19:13, the apostle John wrote about the vision God showed him regarding the glorious second coming of Jesus, and he wrote, "… and his name is called *The Word of God.*"

Back to when I heard the bad news from the nurse after the CT scan of my body, God through His Word in Psalm 112:1, 7, was saying to me that He protects people who *fear* Him and He's there with them in time of need. We're not supposed to be afraid because our heart is *fixed* in the Lord. That means, during difficult times, our heart is connected to God's heart. To our Father's heart, that's how personal He is with us. And that's how we make it when we go through difficult times.

And you know what? That's exactly what happened to me. When I heard the voice of the Lord and the meaning of these Bible verses, this peace that I couldn't explain came upon me, and I didn't worry anymore. It's like the bad news instantly were gone. Had I not had this peace from the Lord, I don't know how I would have managed to go through that day.

When we believe in the Lord Jesus, we know deep down within us that He is the Almighty God, and we have this assurance that everything is in His hands, and that He knows about everything from the smallest to the greatest thing we go through. We shouldn't worry but instead, trust in Him.

When we trust Him, He then comes and fills us with His peace, as it says in Philippians 4:7, "And the peace of God, that passeth all understanding, shall keep your hearts and minds through Christ Jesus."

This peace from above is able to help us overcome even the worst bad news, because He is the Almighty God, and with Him, all things are possible.

In Jeremiah 30:26–27, we read where God told the prophet, "Behold, I am the Lord God, the God of all flesh. Is there anything too hard for me?" Indeed nothing is too hard for Him. All things are possible with Him, and nothing can stop the Lord from intervening in our lives, except ourselves when we don't believe in Him, when we don't trust Him and reject Him, and cast Him out of our lives. But when we do trust in Him, God will come and bring deliverance.

As I went through this bad experience with this illness, the Lord gave me hope and "the peace that passeth all understanding." At times I would ask myself, "Is there something wrong with me? Why am I not worrying about all this illness?" Well, I wasn't worrying because God had given me His peace which was beyond what I could comprehend.

In 1 Timothy 1:1, the apostle Paul wrote, "He is our *hope*". Not only did the Lord give me peace while I was going through this illness, He also gave me hope. And just as the peace from above is beyond our understanding and so important, the hope from above is *life*.

If you don't have the Lord Jesus, and you go through a difficult time as I did, having received such bad news, or if you happen to experience another type of difficult challenge in your life, you will experience the devastation of *hopelessness*. Without the hope from above, hopelessness will settle in your mind and in your heart, and that comes from the enemy.

A person filled with hopelessness will begin to shut down. That's why hopelessness brings death, but the hope from above is life, knowing that the Lord Jesus has everything in His hands. And having Him, you will also have this feeling: That you are not alone.

This hope from the Lord Jesus is important to have at all times in our lives, in good times and in bad, and by that we don't mean only during an illness such as cancer, but of course when other problems or challenges exist. There are people who worry about making their next payment for their home, providing food for their family, whether they will have a job in the near future. Others worry about an addiction, or those who have to deal with depression. There are all kinds of challenges in this life, the list is long.

That's why we need to have the hope that comes from the Lord. And if we have this hope, which is life, we'll be able to overcome any challenge, and some of them can be like huge mountains that are impossible to go through. But with the Lord, who is able to do all things, we'll be able to overcome.

The Lord is able to provide a way for us where there is no way out of those difficult problems we may face. So, no matter what it is that we are dealing with, we must have hope in the Lord, and having the hope and peace from above, we will experience victory no matter what we face in life.

Going back to the urologist, his nurse had called me and gave me a date to meet with him after he had reviewed the results of the CT scan. That's the same man would also perform the surgery to remove my kidney.

And so towards the end of December, I met him in his office, and right there he showed me the picture of my lungs. Some of these "things" were big, and others were small, but there were many.

This doctor told me that he had a great deal of experience with cancer as well, and he knew of course I had been coughing, and he asked, "Do you still cough?"

I said, "Yeah."

"Well," he said, "those are cancerous nodules. Often cancer from the kidneys travels and goes to other places. The most common place that kidney cancer will travel is the lungs." And so he said very unequivocally, "You have cancer in your lungs also."

And that was another devastating time in my life. Tears came down. I couldn't believe what I was hearing! Worse yet, right there, I saw on the computer screen how bad my lungs looked. It was terrible! I can't describe how bad I felt, only that I had reached the depths of despair again when I saw what was happening to me. The doctor looked at me and saw my tears, and without saying anything, he pointed his finger first upward, toward God. Next he pointed toward my wife, and finally he pointed toward himself and finally said, "You have support."

In other words, I could depend on God, my wife, and on him. I knew his intentions were good of course, to make me feel better. He was trying to encourage me, and it's good to have the support of people around us, relatives, friends, and so on, but I knew also that in the condition I was, only the Lord Jesus could give me real support and strength to go on. He is the only One who knows everything there is to know about suffering because He suffered Himself unbearably in the hands of the ungodly Roman soldiers and on the cross, and was able also to deliver me from cancer.

As I finished my meeting with the doctor and walked out of his office with my wife, I went to the scheduling nurse outside his office. She scheduled me for a meeting with the cancer doctor in the same hospital on another day. And right there as I was waiting, the peace of the Lord came upon me again, and the pain in my heart eased. My tears dried up, and I just knew the Lord was with me, standing right next to me.

And though I had peace, still the heaviness of the bad news was weighing down on me. It's the strangest thing that happens when we go through this kind of a situation like hearing dooming words about our very life, especially from someone we consider to be an expert, such as the doctor who in my case was an experienced urologist and a surgeon. Words given to us that describe that our health has some serious problems, causes some psychological things to happen also. I could feel things were not the same, not only physically. I couldn't pinpoint what it was, I couldn't describe it. There are things we just don't know exactly how they work inside of us. It's a mystery how we are made.

As a human being, I was experiencing this sadness while I had peace in my heart, a strange mix. God was supporting my weak human side. Through this peaceful, reassuring voice that was rising from deep within me, the Lord was telling me that everything would be okay, and I knew I needed to trust in Him with all my heart—and not on my feelings from where fear and worries would come through.

The urologist's office indeed set me up with the cancer doctor, who showed me again on the screen the nodules in my lungs, reaffirming it was cancer. She didn't say a whole lot, only that I had to see her again after the removal of my kidney. We left her office with a lot of pain in my heart about all this knowing that the cancer was not only in my left kidney but also in my lungs.

But you know, the peace of the Lord is with us during the most difficult times of our lives, and also in good times. But during good times we don't think much about it. We take it for granted. During difficult times, it is then that we need the Lord most and it is then that His presence becomes more real. That reminds me of the words of the apostle Paul, who said he had this pain in his flesh that felt like a thorn in his side, which according to him, it came from Satan.

Three times he asked the Lord to take it away, and God responded, "My grace is sufficient for thee, for *my strength is made perfect in weakness*" (2 Cor. 12:9). You see, God didn't heal Paul, but He gave him strength and peace to continue his work of spreading the Gospel. Also, through this pain, Paul drew closer to God, and that's the best part.

As I sought God in prayer knowing the condition I was in, I knew that as He gave Paul strength and peace to overcome the difficult time in his life, and the hope he needed to continue doing the work of the Lord, I knew also that He would do the same thing for me. God is the same today as He was then, and He would do the same to anyone who seeks Him in prayer and believes in Him.

And very often, I thought about these precious and life-sustaining gifts of *peace* and *hope* that I received from Him during those very difficult times, and then I would also think: *How do people who don't trust in God, or others who have rejected His Holy Son Jesus, how do they manage to go through the same experience like I was with this terrible illness? How do they go about carrying this awesome burden of an incurable illness alone? How do they manage the difficult times?*

I concluded that they must have a far more difficult time than I did because, without the peace of the Lord, a person is really suffering inside in ways that cannot be adequately described. But worse yet, people without the Lord have no hope. And sooner or later, hopelessness takes over, and hopelessness *will bring death.* That's what happens.

But I praise and thank God that by His grace, I came to know Jesus many years ago, the One who had suffered on the cross in an unbearable way, and He was able to help me through my suffering. And He will also help all those who are suffering in this life, all those who call upon Him in faith.

Not only does the Lord Jesus know all there is to know about suffering, as God, He has every situation, no matter how difficult it may be, in His hand, and He can truly help. And as He gave me the strength, the hope, and the peace to continue through this difficult time, He will do the same for you.

Most of my life, I had sought the Lord God in prayer, offering praise and thanksgiving for all things, lifting up the needs of my family, relatives, friends, and certainly my own continually. But when danger showed up through those original blood tests that had shown something was wrong with me and through all the other tests that had followed, and the MRI that revealed the kidney tumor, the Lord became my continual shelter and my refuge. With every bit of bad news that I was given, my prayer was becoming more intense. I was seeking God many times during the day and speaking His promises to myself, reminding myself what God had promised in His Living Word.

The more I sought the Lord through prayer, and the more I studied the Bible, the stronger my faith became, just as it says in Paul's epistle to the Romans, "So then faith cometh by hearing, and hearing by the word of God" (Rom. 10:17). And that is absolutely true. As I was seeking with fervor the Word of God, I began to *expect* a miracle from God, to heal my kidney before surgery. After all, God's promises are true, right?

The Surgery

On January 12, 2016, I got up early and prayed. I asked the Lord to be with me and to protect me during surgery, and also I reminded Him again of His promises He made in the Bible. Soon after that, my wife and I went to the hospital, arriving there at five thirty in the morning. It was a very cold January morning here in Indiana, and as soon as we arrived, the nurses started the preparation by hooking me up to an IV and doing all the other things that were needed so I'd be ready for the surgery that would follow an hour and half later.

About a half hour before the surgery time, the urologist/ surgeon walked in and said, "Greg, are you ready?"

I said, "Yes, I am."

Then he said, "You know, today we need all the power we can get. Would you please say a prayer?"

Immediately he joined hands with the two nurses, and of course, my wife and I joined them. And I prayed again, asking the Lord to grant the doctor strength, to guide his hands, and to give him wisdom to know what to do because he was about to go in my body to remove my left kidney. I asked the Lord to be present during the surgery time, and I asked in the *name of Jesus*, believing He had heard me, because I felt His great peace in my heart again.

When we ask in the name of Jesus and with faith, He always hears us. In the gospel of John, we read, "And whatsoever ye shall ask in *my name*, that will I do, that the Father may be glorified in the Son. If ye shall ask any thing in my name, I will do it" (John 14:13–14). He means what He says.

Sometime prior to all this, I was with this doctor in his office. I don't know how, but the subject of religion came up. He had told me that he was not a Christian. I told him that I believed in Jesus, the Son of God, and that Jesus, I told him, was the only way to heaven. So I witnessed to him. And I began to tell him more about the Lord when I sensed at some point he was a little bit uncomfortable.

I asked, "Should I continue?"

And he told me, "Don't worry about me Greg, I'm okay."

And so, when he came into the prep room that day, he knew I was a follower of Jesus, and yet he asked me to pray. That gave me great peace in my heart. It didn't matter that he was not a Christian because God is able to speak through any mouth, and He can use any person. I knew the Lord was there with me, and He was encouraging me through this man. And that again gave me the peace I needed at the right time, the peace that comes only from Him.

Prayer with faith brings miracles, and God wants to hear our prayer. Without prayer, the Lord cannot act on our behalf because our prayer is a *sign* of our faith. The apostle Paul said in his first epistle to the Thessalonians, "Pray without ceasing" (1 Thess. 5:17). Therefore, we must *not* stop praying.

So then, it is only through prayer that God acts on our behalf, and through prayer, He will remove any obstacle that stands before us.

Back to the prep room again. Remember, I had mentioned earlier that I was praying all those weeks for the Lord to heal my kidney before the surgery? Well, I was expecting a miracle. I was expecting the doctor would find my kidney healed when he would go into my body, I believed that with all my heart. So before the doctor left the prep room, after I finished praying, I told him, in front of my wife so that I would have a witness. I said, "Doc, when you get in there and see that my kidney is healthy, don't remove it." He looked at me kind of bewildered and said, "Okay. I will not remove it if it's okay."

And so he left. Shortly thereafter, they finished the prep work and one of the nurses placed this breathing mask on my face, and I don't remember anything else.

The surgery lasted four hours. I woke up because a nurse was kind of shaking me in this other room they had put in after surgery, saying, "Greg, wake up. Greg, wake up." This happened three or four times. "Greg, wake up."

Finally I woke up and instantly, I felt this extraordinary pain in my abdomen, I placed my hands over it and I said, "Oh, my stomach." Of course it wasn't my stomach. It was the cutting inside and out of my body. But the pain was so strong that I passed out.

When I woke up sometime later—and I don't know how much time had passed—this extraordinary pain I had experienced earlier, it was down to a fraction, a level I could handle. You see, the Lord removed the pain from me, and I could handle what was left of it. God was with me during surgery and in this room where they had put me in afterward, because He is a God of compassion who cares about us, and no matter what we go through or where we may be, He is right next to us.

While in my recuperating room, the nurse made sure I knew I had access to additional doses of morphine anytime I needed it by simply squeezing this little rubber ball that was placed to my left as I was laying in the bed. She told me I could use this painkiller as many times as I wanted to. It appeared to me that they wanted me to use morphine as much as possible, and I couldn't understand the purpose of that.

I asked, "How often?"

"As often as you want, but only after every ten-minute increments" she said.

But you know the Lord had brought the pain to a level I was able to bear of what was left of that original terrible experience. And so I didn't press the rubber ball to get morphine in my system because I didn't believe it was good for me, and I really didn't need.

But every time the nurse would come to see me, she would say, "You're not using morphine."

And I would reply, "I really don't want it. I am okay."

She would respond, "You need to use it because you'll get better sooner."

I didn't buy that. The Lord is my healer, and He didn't need morphine to complete the healing in my body.

Not only was the Lord taking away the pain from me, He was giving me strength. Within hours after surgery, I got up, with difficulty, and I walked in my room that afternoon. The next day, I walked many times, morning and afternoon, all through this long hallway. The Lord gave me strength to get up from bed, though it was very painful at the beginning as I was putting a lot of pressure on my abdomen muscles while trying to get up, but it became increasingly better with every hour that was passing.

The truth is: The Lord is the source of our strength and of our very own breath every day of our life, and without Him, not only we could not possibly get up from our bed, we would be without life. And so often, we take all that for granted, and we don't thank Him enough for what He gives us every single minute, hour and each day. But we do come to appreciate the precious gifts of strength, good health, and our very life the most when we end up in the hospital with some kind of a problem.

That afternoon, the same day of the surgery, the surgeon came into my room and told me he had to remove my kidney because it was full of cancer. "That's what the biopsy revealed," he said.

I thanked him and said, "I understand".

Keep Trusting in Him

So the Lord didn't heal my kidney before surgery, even though I had prayed with all my heart asking Him to heal me. I went to surgery that day on January 12, 2016, expecting to hear the doctor say, "Your kidney was okay. I didn't have to remove it." But that didn't happen. It turned out to be full of cancer. What happened? Didn't God hear my prayer? After all, I was praying with *faith* and with *expectation*, believing I would get a miracle. Why then didn't He heal me?

The answer: It was not the right time. Yes, He heard me, I believe that with all my heart. When we believe in the Lord and trust in Him, anytime we open our mouth and call upon Him with faith, He does hear our prayers.

If He did not answer your prayer after you have fervently prayed, He is telling you to continue *trusting* and *waiting*, as we talked about it earlier at another section in this book. He wants you to continue trusting in Him, without murmuring and anger, like it was with me, where even though I had prayed with faith, He didn't answer my prayer. God knew what needed to be done, and always has the right time. He knows when it would be the right time to answer our prayer. That's the moment that will be the best for us and bring glory and honor for His own Holy name.

Now I know even more so, that it was indeed the right thing that God didn't heal me before surgery, because many opportunities arose for witnessing after the surgery that have touched the hearts of many people and brought glory to Him. He had a purpose and a *plan* that day, as He always has a plan for all of us, at all times, young and old.

And so I want to encourage you. If you're praying about something that's important to you—like a family issue, your finances, a failing business where you are about to lose everything, a job that is ending, or about this addiction that's drawing you like a giant magnet and you can't pull away from it, or about an illness—whatever it is, if you're praying with faith and believing in His promises found in His Word, you need to know the Lord has heard you. And He always does hear us.

If you didn't get an answer to your prayer when you had expected it, but rather *silence,* the silence is your answer. He's telling you to learn to *trust* in Him, to be *patient* and to have *faith* in Him.

Don't lose your hope. God didn't forget about you or ignore you. He didn't push you off to the side. No, but again, He does have His own timing. And in His time, He will bring the perfect solution to your problem, a miracle, and that's always the perfect solution. God will provide a *way* when everybody else in the world would tell you there is no way out, not possible for you to get out of your situation, but don't listen to unbelieving voices, with Him *all things* are possible, and His name is Jesus.

In the book of Jeremiah, we read where God spoke to him, "Then came the word of the Lord unto Jeremiah, saying, Behold, I am the Lord, the God of all flesh: is there anything too hard for me?" (Jer. 32:26–27).

Indeed nothing is too big or too hard for the Almighty God, who created everything visible and invisible, the heavens, and the earth. Who is able to "count the stars in heaven and to call ALL of them by their name" (Ps. 147:4). If you think about all this that God can do, surely it will fill your heart with astonishment and hope because you will know it is nothing for Him to bring a miracle in your life, regardless how big the mountain may be that you are facing right now. Don't even worry about it, but "cast all your care upon Him (Jesus); for He cares for you" (1 Peter 5:7). And that's what God is telling you right now!

Two days after surgery, I left the hospital, and I went home, able to walk. And within three or four days, I was working and doing the things I normally do. The Lord again gave me strength. And there was peace in my heart, even though my kidney was out, my lungs still had a serious problem. Because of this peace, I kind of forgot everything that was against me. I went about taking care of my family and my business without pain or any sort or discomfort. And that's a miracle. The Lord had given me the strength I needed.

I forgot about the awful pain I had felt inside my body after surgery, and again I forgot about cancer. I didn't even think about it. My trust in the Lord took away any worrying from me. I had this peace that was from above. God Almighty was there with me, helping me and giving me strength so I was able to move and do the things I needed to do.

We read a little further in the Bible about this strength where it says, "And there appeared an angel unto Him from heaven, strengthening Him" (Luke 22:43). This was when the Lord Jesus knew the time was near for His horrendous passion, His suffering. He went into this garden, as we read in the Gospels, with His disciple and He told them to wait for Him, and He moved a little bit further away and began to pray. And being God, He knew the extent of His suffering He had to go through, but as man, Jesus agonized over this horrific suffering that was about to come upon Him. But it says in Scripture that an angel of God was strengthening Him.

You see, the Lord God who was strengthening Jesus at that time of great need, when He, as man needed strengthening, was also the same who was strengthening me, and is the same God who will strengthen you, if you call upon Him during this difficult time in your life. God will send His angel to strengthen you, don't worry. We often lose our strength like it happened to me after surgery, but the Lord is there to renew our strength so that we may continue in life.

Strength, peace, and hope were the most important things I needed, and I received those things from Him during those difficult times of my life, even from the beginning when I found out about this cancer that was in my kidney.

A week after my surgery, I saw the cancer doctor again, who now had the biopsy results of the tumor they took out of my left kidney. She told me that the cancer from my kidney, under the microscope, has shown to be very aggressive. And she showed me again on the computer screen how my lungs looked at the time. She seemed to be very worried, but she didn't say a lot about my condition or future options to follow, but right away she said she highly recommended that I have a second opinion about the cancer in my lungs. And so she told me that the nurse who makes the appointments would make contact with the Indiana University Medical Center in Indianapolis. She emphasized that she highly suggested that I see this doctor who specialized in kidney related cancer, to whom she had sent other patients. And indeed they made an appointment for me. I was supposed to see this doctor on February 12, exactly one month after the surgery.

But by the grace of God, I continued doing my work as though nothing had happened. The Lord again had taken any worry out of me and replaced it with His peace, which was so important and reassuring that it removed any thoughts about the cancer. Many times I would ask myself as I wrote earlier, "*Why am I not worrying? Is there something wrong with me?*" I knew what I had in my lungs, and yet I was not worrying. It was as though nothing had happened. And that's the peace that comes only from the Almighty God.

No matter what we go through, if we trust in Him, He will make sure we have His peace and hope because He truly cares for us as a true Father, and He loves us. In fact, He loves us so much that, according to Scripture, He gave His only begotten Son to die on the cross for our sins according to John 3:16. There is no measure possible that we may use to figure out His great and unconditional love for us. And if we only trust in Him, He will be right there with us to comfort us and to carry us in His arms when we cannot even move sometimes due to the enormity of the challenges we may face in this life.

My Problem Was Bigger

The time came for the first visit to the Indiana University Medical Center. On February 12, 2016, I drove with my wife to Indianapolis to meet with this doctor for the first time. His specialty again was in kidney associated cancer. A few days before the date of the appointment, one of his nurses had called and told us that this doctor takes a lot of time with each patient. She said we should be prepared to wait for a long time to see him.

And so it happened that we waited almost two hours in the waiting area and another hour in this exam room. But it was all worth it because eventually he came in. He sat down and spent an hour and fifteen minutes. It was toward the end of the day on a Friday and by the time we were finished, we were the only ones left in that big place.

He explained to me in the best possible way what I had in my lungs, and for the first time, I came to realized how bad my situation was, how really bad my lungs were. I realized that this cancer was a terrible thing because he said kidney-related cancer is like a moving target.

"We don't know where it may show up" he said. In your case, he told me, "It showed up in your lungs." It was very difficult for me to sit down and listen to all he was telling me, to absorb all the things he was describing about this cancer. And I had a lot of questions.

Towards the end, I asked him to tell me how long did I have left: "How long does it take from the time one is diagnosed with this kind of cancer until the end?" I said.

I don't know he replied. And I said, "Sure you do, you have been doing this work for a long time and you have seen many people. Then he said, "Well, you know, everyone's different. Some have a longer time; others have less time. But it's about twenty to twenty-four months."

When I heard that, despair filled my heart. It's very difficult to hear something so terrible, such bad news, especially from someone who knows about this particular illness I had. It is difficult to overcome the words I heard. Even though it's good to hear the truth, this truth about the condition of my lungs, was very difficult for me to handle.

In the Bible we read, "Death and life are in the power of the tongue" (Prov. 18:21). That means the things we say could affect us and the people around us either in positive or a negative way, depending what we say. By the words we speak, we can either bring condemnation or encouragement upon another person. That's why we need to be careful how we talk to people. We need to be careful especially, how we talk to our young sons and daughters because, when we speak condemning words, they will stay with them for a long time. It has the same effect, of course, when we hear condemning words from somebody as it was the case with me, from an expert like the doctor. Those things go deep into our heart. I don't know how exactly to explain it, but something happened inside of me when I heard the death sentence.

Something happened that I cannot explain. I couldn't understand what was it, but it was not good even though I had been praying, and God was with me. There was worry, fear and anxiety. I found myself in the depths of despair again after the doctor had told me that it could be anywhere between twenty to twenty-four months. It was a difficult thing to accept.

I left his office in really bad shape that day. I will never forget February 12, 2016, knowing I had so little time ahead of me. And for a while, the devil was doing a great job on me with his usual tricks by bringing all those bad thoughts of condemnation and hopelessness like, you are done, there is no hope, nobody can save you, and even a vision of my own funeral came right in front of me. The purpose of all that was to destroy me by filling my mind with thoughts of hopelessness, to move me away from my faith and hope I had in the Living God. That's what the devil brings when we are in difficult times, and we need to be aware of his devices and resist him by being grounded firmly in the truth found in the Word of God. The Lord reminds about it, "… Resist the devil, and he will flee from you' (James 4:7).

But thank God, as I continued on the highway going back home, the Lord gave me a peace that flooded my being. And I wondered, *how could I possibly be so peaceful at such a time when I knew my time was limited?*

It was because of Jesus, a miracle, and it came at the right time. The Lord Jesus always shows up at the right time to give us what we need, and peace was what I needed most as I was coming back from Indianapolis that day. But the Lord gave me also hope to be able to continue. And for all this, I give Him all the glory, because truly I made the rest of the trip back home by His grace.

I got up the next day, February 13, and I started writing down verses that talked about hope, life, deliverance, and healing, about fifty of them. And I began to memorize them. I began to speak those verses to myself when I was at home or in my car. I would speak aloud and kept repeating them many times during the day. The more I immersed myself in the Word of God, the greater even became the peace and the hope in my heart. Just as I wrote in another section, when we study the Word of God with passion, when we immerse ourselves in His Word, Jesus comes in us and He brings those priceless gifts when we need them most in our life: Peace and hope.

After so many years that I have been studying the Bible, I knew this time, more than ever, that the Word of God was alive. In 2 Timothy 3:16, the apostle Paul wrote, "All scripture is given by inspiration of God." And the apostle Peter also wrote in 2 Peter 1:21, "For the prophecy came not in old time by the will of men, but holy men of God spoke as they were moved by the Holy Spirit." You see, all the Words in the Bible came from the Living God, they are His Words, and they are Living Words.

After I had visited this doctor at the Indiana University Medical Center on that day on February 12, 2016, and had received the bad report, I knew my only hope was the Lord. Nobody and nothing else was able to heal me, but I knew He could. And so I sought Him with all my heart through His Word.

As we study the Word with zeal, we hear it and it goes in our heart. And that's when faith comes from, the kind of faith that causes us to begin to *expect* a miracle. And expecting a miracle is what pleases the Lord. God sees and hears everything. And when He sees us being so serious that we have reached a point to *expect* to receive from Him, God moves on our behalf, because the expectation of a miracle shows to Him that we truly believe who He says He is, and further, we show that we believe He is *able* to deliver what He had promised in His Word.

Are you suffering from any illness right now? Are you wrestling with an addiction? Are you facing a challenge so big that it looks like a mountain? Do you have problems you cannot resolve—financial, family, business, or job related—that are standing right there in front of you? I can tell you from experience that, if you immerse yourself in the Living Word of God, seeking Him with all your heart, He will be standing right there, next to you. You will feel His presence, because He will be giving you strength, peace and hope, just like He did with me, and that's Jesus, the Lord of lords and the King of kings.

At the beginning of this book, we've talked about faith, but it's important to remind ourselves again about this important subject. The apostle Paul wrote about it in his epistle to Hebrews saying, "Now faith is the substance of things hoped for, the evidence of things not seen" (Hebrews 11:1).

So then if you're praying to God with faith, you're *expecting* to receive the things you've asked God to give you, and your faith becomes the *evidence* that you already have the things you can't see and the things you cannot *touch* yet.

Through your faith then, the unseen things will become the things you see and touch. Praying with faith brings miracles.

We must also remember what we wrote again at the beginning of this book. If we don't have faith, our prayers cannot be answered according to Apostle Paul who wrote, "… without faith, it is *impossible* to please Him (God)…" (Hebrews 11:6). It's important therefore, that we have faith in God which shows Him we trust in Him to provide, and that's what will move God to act on our behalf.

But unfortunately, many are trusting and hoping to receive help from people and not God. They seek help by praying to and placing their hope in people, or in man-made things and not in the living God. As a result, they don't receive anything, because it raises the anger of God rather than His favor towards them. In the book of Jeremiah, we read what God said to him about what happens when we trust in people and not in Him,

> "Thus saith the Lord; *cursed* be the man that trusteth in man, and maketh flesh (man) his arm, and whose heart departeth from the Lord. For he shall be like the heath in the desert, and shall not see when good cometh; but shall inhabit the parched places in the wilderness, in a salt land and not inhabited. *Blessed* is the man that *trusteth* in the Lord, and whose hope the Lord is" (Jer. 17:5–7).

And so, if we pray to the living God with faith and with trust in Him, He will provide what we have asked of Him *through* His Son Jesus, and that's why it's important we believe in Jesus. And when we believe in Him we believe in God. When we love Jesus, we love God. And if we do love Jesus, He will be in our lives, and God the Father will love us as well, and He will be in our lives also, as we read, "For the Father himself loveth you, because ye have loved Me, and have believed that I came out from God" (John 16:27). That's how the blessings of God come to us that we have asked of Him in prayer.

On the other hand, we also need to understand that if we don't have the Lord Jesus in our lives, we don't have the Father either. And without God in our life, we cannot expect to receive a miracle when we need it most in difficult times.

In Psalm 147:4 we read, "He (God) tells the number of the stars and He calls them all by their name." Can you believe that? Do you see how awesome God is? Not only is He able to count the stars, He has a name for each one of them. Well, how many stars are there? Can you lift up your head and count them all at night? Impossible. Scientists' estimate there are about one septillion stars (that's the number one followed by twenty-four zeros).

I believe the scientists are way off. But no matter how many stars are up there, the Bible tells us God calls each one of them by its name. That's how powerful God is. Point is: If we believe in His Son Jesus, who died on the cross for our sins, God Almighty who is able to name each one of the stars, will do *whatever* we ask, and He will provide it at the perfect time, and it will be a miracle, because He is the God of miracles. Knowing therefore what God is able to do for us through Jesus, it brings in us this peace that no matter what obstacle or problem is against us, our Heavenly Father is able to remove it.

As I began studying the Word of God with intensity after the meeting with the cancer specialist at the Indiana University Medical Center, and speaking out loud to myself the verses I had written on paper, my faith began to rise in me, just as I remember how my mother, when I was a child back home in Greece, used to make homemade bread. She would work the dough by mixing flour, water, and salt. Then she would put in the yeast. Next, she would cover the whole thing in this wooden box, but we were not allowed to uncover it because it had to be kept warm—just as the Holy Spirit of God warms our heart, when we immerse ourselves in God's Word.

And so, when Mom was not looking, I'd go and look inside, where the dough was and I would see it rising, and that's because of the yeast. Well, that's how I relate to what happened to my faith. The Word of God acted like the yeast that caused the dough to rise because His Word is a living Word, and like the yeast, it caused my faith to rise as well. And I believe with all my heart that is what brought my eventual healing. God is pleased with faith!

And if you are suffering right now from something that's been consuming you through fear and worry, whatever it may be please take Jesus and His Word seriously. He will give you hope and peace, and above all, He will deliver you from the grip of this thing that's pulling you down.

My next appointment to see the doctor at the IU Medical Center was on February 25, 2016. That morning, I left home alone this time, and drove toward Indianapolis while praying for nearly the entire two-and-a-half-hour drive, I felt the presence of God in the car with me. And like during those other times prior to this morning, I was asking God for a miracle, and I was *expecting* to receive one. I couldn't wait to see the doctor and hear the good report from the tests, the miracle I was hoping for, which would be manifested through the result of the tests, proving I was healed.

When I arrived at the medical center, I walked anxiously toward the part of the hospital where I would have the CT scan of my chest, abdomen, and pelvis first. After that, I was supposed to walk to another place of the hospital where I would have an MRI test of my head. This is the noisy machine where you lay in this tube, all stretched out, for about thirty-five minutes. And after that, I was supposed to have the blood tests at another part of the hospital. And in the afternoon, after the doctor had all the results from these tests, he would come and see me in his office.

So I went to have the CT scan, and at about ten thirty, I was finished with that. I moved to the next place for the MRI. I had about an hour before they would call me in the room for the test. I sat near this large window waiting, where the warm sun was coming through on this cold February day. I was relaxing there for a few minutes when the nurse came out and called my name.

"Greg Doublas?"

I said, "I'm Greg."

She continued, "The person before you didn't show up, would you like to take the test now?"

I thought, Why not? I'll get it over with sooner, and I'll relax a little bit more without interruption for a while before I would have the blood tests.

So I went in to take the MRI test, laying in this tube with my ears plugged up, trying to endure the noise while the machine took a picture of the inside of my head as the doctor wanted. Thank God, soon it was finished, and I got dressed. I went out, and this time I went closer to this other part of the compound where I would be having the blood tests. Actually I was a little closer to the doctor's office as well. And so I was hoping to relax there for a while, having time alone with the Lord and spending some time with my other favorite thing, watching the national news on my cell phone.

But the minute I sat down, my phone rang. I noticed it was from an area code I didn't recognize, and usually, if I see an area code I'm not familiar with, I don't answer the phone call. But this time I did.

The instant I said "hello," this voice came across, "Are you Greg?"

I said, "Yes."

He said, "I am Kirk, and I called to pray for you."

I didn't know this man, I had never met him before.

He said, "Is it okay to pray for you?"

I said, "Oh … yes." (Prayer should always be welcomed. It is the best thing someone can do for us, because the Bible is teaching us in James 5:16, "… The effectual fervent prayer of a righteous man availleth much." And I knew deep in my heart that this man on the phone, was a man of God).

So he began to pray in an awesome way. He began calling upon the Lord for my healing and asking Him to give me hope and peace and strength to cope with what I was going through. He even asked the Lord to provide the finances to pay for the expenses of the tests and the doctor. His prayer brought tears to my eyes.

When he finished, I felt great. I felt the presence of the Lord even more so in my life. I knew that I knew, that the Lord had sent this man to pray for me, and the time was perfect. I also thought for sure I would hear about my miracle today.

Had I taken the MRI when I was supposed to, I would have missed his call. Like I said earlier, the man who was supposed to be before me to take the MRI test didn't show up, so I took the MRI test earlier. And thus it turned out to be the perfect time to receive this man's call. But also it was before I would see the doctor from whom I was expecting to hear the good news.

Only God can work out things like that. And that's because He has everything in His hand. I knew after I finished talking to this man that God had sent him. As I mention earlier, I never met him or knew him from before. But it was a man who obeyed the Lord and called me to pray for me. I had this peace upon me, and I knew the Lord was on my side.

He who commands this awesome universe had *remembered* me, and had sent this man to pray for me during this critical time. Do you see how personal and how caring our God is? And of course, I was now more confident that He would bring me the miracle I was waiting. That I would receive good news from the doctor when I would see him next.

Soon after that, I went to have the blood test, and after that, I was supposed to see the doctor and hear the good news, right? Well that's what I was expecting on that day,

February 25, 2016. But the Lord had something different in His mind for me that day. What was it?

WAITING ANXIOUSLY

I finished taking the blood tests, and I again moved to another area where I waited for the nurse to take me to the exam room. I was very anxious. The time came finally when they call me, and I settled in the exam room waiting to see the doctor, still a little anxious, waiting for the big news. About an hour or so later, the doctor showed up.

He sat down, looked at me, and said, "Greg, I have bad news for you. The CT scan has shown that the nodules in your lungs have multiplied. The bigger nodules that were there have become even bigger. And you have a lot more of these things in your lungs now."

Obviously the doctor had compared the results of the tests I had taken that morning to the CT scans from December 2015, about two months earlier, and they had arrived at the conclusion that my health had deteriorated. When the doctor finished giving me the bad news, it felt like a giant invisible fist hit me in my abdomen, and this sound came out of me, "Ah …" It was as though I had received an actual physical blow to my stomach. Oh, the pain in my heart!

Here I was expecting to hear good news about my health, a miracle of healing. Instead I heard devastating news. This was the worst time in my life, worse than when I first heard about what was in my lungs and the cancer in my kidney, two or more months earlier. This was far worse because I went there expecting a miracle. After all, I was in prayer on my knees all the days, and God had even sent this man to call me, and because of that, my expectation became even greater to hear good news, and what did I hear? The nodules had multiplied. My condition was getting worse.

I was devastated.

I began thinking about the time I had left, and right there at the doctor's office, I learned what it really means to be in the *depths of despair*. It's a strange feeling or rather a bunch of things that are happening inside the body that bring you to utter desperation and hopelessness, even though I was in prayer. For a little while, everything had ceased in my mind. I just sat there in that office. But then a little miracle. The Lord intervened again to help me overcome this great burden of defeat that was all over me by giving me strength again.

This strength that had come upon me was like the strength at other times. It was from the Lord, and not from me, because I didn't have anything left in me after the bad news. And I knew then, that this strength that had come upon me *was the result of this man's prayer* whom God had sent to pray for me, a few hours earlier. I knew the Lord was answering his prayer he had prayed. And I could also see the Lord's faithfulness, compassion, and love by being there with me in the doctor's office during this truly bad time. God had sent this man to pray so that I receive help and be able to bear these devastating news. God knew all about it.

Through this strength the Lord gave me, I spoke out loud to myself saying, "I feel like the Israelites who had left Egypt and walked all the way to the Red Sea, and there they stopped. They had nowhere to go, but God had provided a way for them."

Of course we read the story in the Old Testament where it says the Israelites heard Pharaoh's horses approaching. Pharaoh had changed his mind, and was coming for them. Fear gripped their hearts because they had nowhere to go. No way out. The Red Sea in front and Pharaoh approaching from behind.

The Israelites began crying out to Moses for help, and he, a man of faith said, "Fear ye not, stand still, and see the salvation of the Lord, which He will show to you today" (Exodus 14:13).

And what did the Lord do for His people? He provided a *new way* for them, where there was no way out. God split the mighty Red Sea and dried the bottom, and they walked on dry land. An impossible thing, humanly speaking, but God made it possible, and that's a true story. You see, with God, all things are possible because His wisdom and power have no end.

And so I said to myself out loud again, in front of the doctor, "And God will provide a *way* for me also." The instant I finished saying this, the doctor said, "No, the pill will provide a way for you."

Earlier, he had described to me that, for my type of cancer, there were two pills available from two different pharmaceutical companies. He said I could choose to take one of the two because these two basically did the same thing, but of course as I found out later, had different side-effects. But I didn't listen to what the doctor said, the pill would provide a way for me. I was not going to place my hope on a pill, and despite how bad I felt after I heard his report, my hope was still in the Lord. I was trusting Him to provide the way I needed out of this illness. After these bad news, I knew even more now that only God could save me.

Before I left his office, the doctor gave me a bunch of papers to look over that had the four options for my treatment. I was to choose one of the four and then give them a call. Two of the options were the two different pills I mentioned earlier, and I could choose one or the other. Another option was to go to the hospital for one week, during which they would put this chemical in me through an IV. And then I would take off a week and then come back again another week to get this chemical again. The purpose of that option would be to strengthen my immune system, and in an indirect way, my immune system would then slow down the cancer. The fourth option was to participate in a new study supported by a certain pharmaceutical company. My doctor was directing that study.

I asked about the side effects of being part of his study for the type of cancer I had, and he said, "Well, we don't know what the side effects may be. But a doctor will follow you closely."

Now let me say again. It's a mystery how we are made and what happens inside when we get a death sentence. Unless you've experienced that, there no way you can understand how it feels. It does something inside of us. I believe that a man or a woman who hears such news begins to die inside. Physically, we may seem to be all right and may tell other people who may ask us about our health, "I am fine, or I am doing okay." But inside, this devastation brings an enormous damage. I cannot describe it, but I knew something was happening inside me, and it wasn't good. The minute I got into my car, tears began to come down.

And as I was driving home toward the end of the day from the Indiana University Medical Center which is near downtown Indianapolis, I had to drive through heavy traffic on secondary streets, then onto major highways, 65 and 70-East, and then onto the bypass. And then finally to I-69 heading north toward Fort Wayne. But this water that was coming down from my eyes was causing a problem with my driving. I couldn't see. With one hand, I was driving, holding the steering wheel, and with the other, I was wiping my eyes. And this continued for some time. I wasn't crying physically, but I guess I was crying inside.

And I will repeat again what is said in Proverbs 18:21, "Death and life are in the power of the tongue." When we hear the words of the bad news from a person of authority it does a lot of damage. In my case, it went straight into my heart and brought a massive pain.

And so those tears continued as I drove through the heavy traffic, but as the stress from the heavy traffic began to slow down when I finally reached I-69, I heard this voice rising out from inside of me that said, "You're not alone." I knew it was the Lord because it brought the peace that I knew.

As I wrote earlier, when God speaks, no matter which way He may choose to speak, two things always happen:

1. You know who spoke because of this witness in you.
2. And you know exactly what He said. There is no doubt or confusion.

In that same moment, He also spoke these words to me, "Cast it out." But with these words, there was also an unspoken message that let me know of what I was supposed to do next.

I was to cast out the spirit of *grief* and *sorrow* (to tell the devil to leave from me. You see, Jesus has given us the authority to cast out demons. In the Gospel of Mark 16:17, we read, "And these sings shall follow them that believe; in my name shall they cast out devils ..."). Grief and sorrow are part of the devils gifts, and they come to us in difficult times, when we are most vulnerable, so that we may give up, begin to feel sorrow for ourselves. The devil wants to discourage us, and have us believe there is nothing left for us, that there is no hope. And if we allow that to happen, hopelessness will follow next, and that will bring a complete defeat. That's when people die.

And so, I said what the Lord told me to say, "In the name of Jesus Christ of Nazareth, I cast you out of me." When I said that, the tears stopped, and the peace I knew from before, came upon me again.

You see, the enemy wants us to lose the battle. That made me think again about people who do not know the Lord Jesus, and I thought, when they go through such devastating times in their life, how do they manage? Here I was praying with all my heart, trusting and believing in God, and I really had a hard time. How do people make it without God, those who don't believe in Him?

I concluded that they don't make it. When you are facing a challenge you know you cannot overcome, you begin to die inside because the hope from above is not there, and that brings hopelessness, which in turn brings death.

On the other hand, when you have the Lord Jesus in your life, He gives you this hope from Him that no one else can give you. And that hope is life. It gives you this assurance inside that all things will turn out to be okay, just as Scripture is teaching us, "And we know that all things work together for good to them that love God, to them who are the called according to His purpose" (Romans 8:28).

Remember what we wrote earlier? When we love Jesus, we love God the Father, and all things will work for good for those who love Him.

In John 14:6, we read where the Lord Jesus told His disciples, "I am the way, the truth and the life. No man comes to the Father but by me." You see, apart from Jesus, there's no way to the Throne of God. But when we know Jesus, we are at the throne of God *through* Him, and when we pray invoking His name, the name of Jesus, God hears us. He is the One who took those tears from me and gave me peace during this difficult time as I was leaving Indianapolis, after I had heard the bad report from the doctor who told me the cancer had multiplied in me. God had given me this peace through faith in the Lord Jesus. A miracle.

I would like to share a little story with you. Perhaps you might have heard it before. It's called "Footsteps in the Sand." In this story, someone described how one time he saw a dream, and in this dream, he saw himself walking on the beach with the Lord. And as a result, he noticed two sets of footprints. He said that many scenes from his life "flashed across the sky," which were corresponding to the footprints on the sand. Sometimes there were two sets of prints, and other times there was one set.

But sadly, during the most difficult times in his life, he noticed one set of footprints and said to the Lord, "You promised me that you would be with me all the time, but I have noticed during the most trying periods of my life there was only one set of footprints. Why when I needed you most you were not there with me?" And the Lord answered, "The times when you saw only one set of footprints, it was then when I was carrying you" (Mary Stevenson, 1936).

You see, the Lord does the same thing every day with all of us, and that's why, without Him, no one can make it alone, especially during trying times. And that day, February 25, 2016, when I received the terrible news from the doctor, I made it because of the Lord Jesus. He was carrying me in His arms.

The Lord who heard me and delivered me from the horrific devastation of the bad news was the same Lord who also had heard David and delivered him out of the hands of king Saul of Israel, who wanted to kill him, as we read,

> "And David spake unto the Lord the words of this song in the day that the Lord had delivered him out of the hand of all his enemies, and out of the hand of Saul. And he said, The Lord is my rock, and my fortress, and my deliverer; The God of my rock; in him will I trust: he is my shield, and the horn of my salvation, my high tower, and my refuge, my savior; thou savest me from violence. I will call on the Lord, who is worthy to be praised: so shall I be saved from mine enemies. When the waves of death compassed me, the floods of ungodly men made me afraid; the sorrows of hell compassed me about; the snares of death prevented me; sorrows: or, cords. In my distress I called upon the Lord, and cried to my God: and he did hear my voice

> out of his temple, and my cry did enter into
> his ears" (2 Sam. 22:1–7).

I want to share with you a few of the many Bible verses that were so important to me during the difficult times I went through:

In Psalm 34:4, it says, "I sought the Lord and He heard me, and delivered me from all my fears." In Psalm 34:17, we read, "The righteous cry, and the Lord hears and delivers them out of all their troubles." Now who are the righteous? The answer is: Those who *truly believe* in the Lord Jesus, those who place their trust upon Him, the true believers. When they cry (pray), the Lord hears them and delivers them from all their troubles. He never fails to hear us.

In Psalm 91:15, it says, "He shall call upon me, and I will answer him. I will be with him in trouble ..." An awesome statement from the Almighty God. And that's what He does. He answers when we call upon Him in our troubles, because He loves those who love His beloved Son Jesus. And that's where the peace that passes all understanding comes from, from Him, by believing in *what* He has promised in His Word.

No matter how difficult a time we're having, or how big the challenges we face in life, the Lord will be right there to deliver us. That's His promise.

New Hope

I immersed myself again in the Word of God, studying the Bible with greater intensity after the bad report I received on that day, February 25th, knowing the Lord was my only hope.

It is very difficult to go through very challenging times as I did, and other people as well, but I will say there is a bright side to all this also. These difficult times can bring us closer to God because we seek Him with all our heart, knowing He is our only hope. We read in Scripture earlier in 1 Chronicles 28:9 where is says, "… If you seek Him He will be found of you." And that's the blessing, and once we find Him, we have this awesome feeling of peace and hope that His presence only brings by knowing, whatever might happen, He will never leave us or forsake us.

I also want to mention here something very special that happened to me one day. As I was seeking God through His Word and prayer, one day the Lord gave me a new verse from His Word that brought this feeling, this assurance that I would be alright. This verse became what I called my *anchor*. It is Psalm 118:17 and it says, "I shall not die, but live, and declare the works of the Lord." This was my special verse because it spoke life upon me, but also it was a confirmation from the Lord that He wanted me to continue spreading the good news of the gospel through the radio program which I had started a few years back, but unfortunately I had to stop for a while.

Getting back to the miracle I was expecting to receive on that day of February 25, 2016, but instead received a very bad report about my lungs, I want to make sure I highlight again this important point: If you have asked in prayer, as I did before coming to see the doctor that day, but you haven't received what you've asked, don't be upset or disappointed.

Don't lose your hope. But rather continue to hope and trust in the Lord, and do not stop praying.

The Lord wants you to learn to trust in Him. He didn't ignore you nor did He forget about you, just as He didn't forget about me. As it was in my case, I was supposed to wait and to continue trusting and hoping in Him, to continue in prayer, and at His time, He did bring my miracle, my healing.

I continued every day studying His Word, and as I wrote earlier, when we have the Word in us, Jesus comes and dwells in us, and faith begins to rise. And despite that cancer was in me, I had peace in my heart. Again, as I wrote earlier in this book, sometimes I would worry if anything was wrong with me, and I would ask myself, *why am I not worrying about this cancer in my lungs?* Well, the answer is, the Lord had given me His peace and the assurance from His Word that I would be alright.

Every day the Word of God was my companion, and I would talk to the Lord about how I felt each day. God wants us to talk to Him. He wants to hear from us, just as our earthly fathers want us to talk to them. I would remind Him about His promises by saying, "Lord God, this is what you said. Since you promised about this or that, then I expect for you to honor your Word." In other words, I talked to Him like a living person right next to me. I felt deep inside of me, that the Lord was pleased when I would remind Him of his promises, when I just talk to Him like a Father. He is pleased when we communicate with Him with simple words coming from our heart.

But many people including those from the "Christian" family, who have this false belief that God used to exist way in the past, and not during these current times. They don't believe in Him. I have heard even regular church goers say, "Oh ... I believe in some higher power" when they attempt to express how they feel about Him. But the Almighty God is not just a hypothetical being, hanging out there somewhere. He is real and alive, and in His hands He holds everything. Believe in Him.

He made this awesome "thing," the cosmos, the heavens and the earth, and everything in them. And in everything He made, there is a breath-taking beauty, and an infinitely higher precision than the finest Swiss watch, or anything man has ever made.

I heard a brilliant nuclear physicist one time on Christian TV, who made this awesome statement regarding this universe, and I am quoting him based on my recollection. He said, "That if a speck of dust was to be added or be removed from this universe, the whole thing would collapse." His statement had utterly left me astonished. I truly don't know if this is correct, but I believe with all my heart that the Almighty God whose wisdom and power are unending, is able beyond any doubt, to accomplish such as thing. But if the statement he made is true, then literally *everything* everywhere exists by the grace of God. Think about it.

In Jeremiah 17:7–8, we read, "Blessed is the man that *trusts* in the Lord, whose *hope* the Lord is, for he shall be as a tree planted by the waters and that spreadeth out her roots by the river, and shall not see when heat comes. But her leaf shall be green. It shall not be careful in the year of drought, neither shall it cease from yielding fruit."

Well, that's what happens to any of us who trusts and hopes in the Lord. We will be like the tree planted by the waters. And just as the tree that's by the waters will always have green leaves, so shall every one of us be who trusts and hopes in the Lord, and dwells in His Word. We shall overcome and will be prospering in the midst of challenging times. When I had the cancer in my lungs, I had peace and hope that everything would be fine, and that's prospering, despite the problem I was facing.

One night after I received those bad news on February 25th, I stayed up late studying those four options for possible treatment I had received from the doctor. I was in my office way past midnight, everybody was sleeping in our home. As I was going over these papers, I was finding that for each one of these options, there was a long list of side effects. In fact, for one of the pills, the last item on the list it said it may even stop my heart. And for every side effect they listed, on the side, in separate column, they noted another medicine the doctor could prescribe to counter the particular side-effect, and the lists went on. I was trying to think what possibly may happen if I were to choose any one of these options, and finally, I asked myself, do I want to gain a few months being alive, and be very sick at the same time?

This proved to be a very difficult question to answer. I didn't know what option of the four to choose, *I didn't know what to do.* Considering everything I had learn from reading these papers the doctor gave me, and from going on-line searching about this cancer, I was still confused. Finally turned again to Jesus who I knew could help me.

I said, "Lord, I'm confused. I really don't know what to do about these options the doctor is proposing." The instant I finished talking, the Lord spoke in a different way this time. Miraculously, He took my mind to a particular verse in the Bible, somehow I saw this verse in my mind. It was in the epistle of James and it said, "All *good* and *perfect* things come from above from the Father of lights" (James 1:17). The Lord spoke through His Word. He gave me direction and helped me to know what to do.

You see, none of those options that were supposed to help me were good for me. These drugs were not from the living God, but from men. A drug we may take that is supposed to help us, but instead makes us sick is not from God. He will not provide the knowledge for a drug that makes you sicker than you are. The Lord is able to provide the knowledge for a drug that would be perfect, a drug that would bring complete healing and peace upon anyone who takes it.

And so I said, "Lord, I'm not taking any of these options. I'm going to trust in you. I *know* you can heal me, but if you don't heal me, *it will be okay with me.*"

God delights when we ask Him. When we seek help and admit our weakness, when we ask from the bottom of our heart. And that's how the Lord hears, intervenes, and brings miracles.

But when we are praying, asking for God's help, we always should allow space for God's will to prevail in our situation. That's why I said to Him, "But if you don't heal me, it will be okay with me." The truth is it's difficult to make that statement. But we have to trust in Him at all times, because He knows what is best for us. For a believer trusting in God completely, it is a win-win situation. If God heals you, it would be great, but if He doesn't, it should be okay also, because you will go to be with the Lord, in the

Kingdome of Heaven and in the presence of the Living God. Where life never ends.

And so don't stop asking God to intervene in your situation, and don't stop trusting in Him no matter how big the problem is. He will bring what you ask of Him because there is nothing but compassion and a love in Him that's far beyond our understanding. And He will provide what you've asked at the right time. Don't stop praying as the apostle Paul encouraged us, "Pray without ceasing" (1 Thessalonians 5:17).

Going back to the night when I was going over the four options the doctor had given me, when I thought about this verse the Lord had directed me, in James 1:17, the confusion turned into peace, and I never called the doctor back. I continued being in God's Word, and trusting His promises and hoping in Him. This expectation for a miracle began to rise in me. It was very real. It was so strong that I could even sense the miracle that was coming as I was getting closer to my next appointment, which was set for April 25, 2016, two months after the previous appointment of February 25th a day I will never forget in my life.

As my next appointment was approaching, hope was also rising in me. I knew something good was happening in me, and that's because I trusted in the Almighty God. And this good feeling, this hope that I will have good news was because of Him, not because of me.

Often those who don't believe are looking for an excuse to justify something that cannot be explained, such as a miracle, trying to attribute an unusual event to one's strength or good genes. But miracles do happen, and Jesus is the reason and not man's ability. And I would encourage you again that no matter what you're going through or how big the challenge you are facing is, have faith and trust in the Lord Jesus.

We all need the Lord because, in so many different ways in this life, we often experience great challenges that completely overwhelm us and leave us with no possible way out. But if we have faith and trust in Him, He will provide a way for us where there seems to be no way and no hope. And so I encourage you to continue to trust and have faith in Jesus, our God, through whom nothing shall be impossible as we read in Luke 1:37.

In the epistle to the Romans, we read about Abraham, the father of faith. God had visited him and told him that he would have a son in a year's time. Abraham believed God, despite the fact that he was one hundred years old and Sarah, his wife, was ninety, way past the age of childbearing. Paul wrote,

> "And being not weak in faith, he considered not his own body now dead when he was about an hundred years old, neither yet the deadness of Sarah's womb. He staggered not at the promise of God through unbelief, but was strong in faith, giving God the glory. And being fully persuaded that what He had promised, He was able also to perform" (Rom. 4:19–21).

Abraham trusted in God and was fully persuaded that God was able to perform what He had promised to him. He didn't think about the problems he was facing—his age, and Sara's, because to a man of faith, the extent of the problem or the challenges, does not matter, because with God everything is possible.

And for you also, no matter what you're going through right now, or how impossible it may be to overcome the problem you are facing, with God everything is possible. Trust in Him.

The Miracle

As the day was approaching for my next visit at the Indiana University Medical Center on April 25, I was becoming increasingly more confident that I would receive a miracle. But it was better that that. I had this assurance in me that I was healed already. All I was waiting for, was the confirmation from the doctor about my healing. And I know beyond any doubt that my time in the Word of God, the hours I spent studying and speaking the Word, was giving me this assurance. The Word of God, which is Jesus according to Revelation 19:13, was healing me because it is a Living Word, and Jesus is the Living God as it is written in 1 John 5:20. Because of the Lord Jesus, I was happy and anxious, and I couldn't wait to see the doctor again and hear the good news of a miracle.

Sunday, April 24, the day before my appointment with the doctor, it was the first day of the Holy Week of Pascha (or Easter) for the Orthodox Church. I went to church to chant (and of course here is another proof that not *only* did I feel like I was already healed, I was able to chant with great strength when I was supposed to be coughing blood, be frail and sick).

Right before the liturgy started, I asked our priest if he had any free time to meet with me sometime on Wednesday (two days after my meeting with doctor), because I was so sure that I would receive the good news of my healing the next day (Monday), I wanted to share with our priest the miracle from the Lord. In other words, I was so confident I was healed that I wanted to make an appointment to talk about it even before I had the confirmation from the doctor. And this faith again came from the Living Word of God, not because of any personal ability or any trait of some sort that was in me. All glory belongs only to the Lord Jesus.

Finally, the big day, Monday, April 25, came and that morning I took off early to go to Indianapolis. As usual, when I arrived I went through the same routine: The CT scans of my chest, abdomen, and my pelvis and then the blood tests. This time I didn't have to do the MRI test for my head because the doctor had determined I was okay there. Plus, I found out later the insurance didn't authorize another MRI within the two-month interval.

I was waiting anxiously, like never before, to hear something great. And I don't know if you ever had this kind of thing happen to you in your life, where you anxiously wait for some great thing to happen to you. It is a special experience, and I don't know how to say it any better. Only the Lord brings those good feelings of happy anxiety, and I was anxious for sure, but it was good anxiety if such a thing exists.

I was filled with hope and expectation that I would hear good news. I could feel it. I knew a miracle was going to happen on that day, April 25, 2016. And so, after I had the blood tests, I was waiting to see the doctor.

And I would like to encourage you dear reader from the bottom of my heart, knowing how hard it is to suffer with something as bad as having an incurable illness, that you would consider devoting yourself to studying the Bible, the Word of God. Memorize verses, and seek it with passion, with a greater desire than you seek food for your physical body, and you will see this faith rising in you as well. The living God that granted me the expectation and the assurance that I was healed through His Word, will do the same for you as well.

No matter what you may be going through now, if you trust in the Lord and dwell in His Word with all your heart, God will provide a miracle for you. He will provide a way for you where there's none in sight. Your faith will rise in you, just like it happened to me. Every word you will read in the Bible is absolutely true. It is God's Word, and His promises are for all those who believe in Christ. And when you take the Word in you, miracles will take place. So trust in the Lord and dwell in His Word. I don't want you to suffer, Jesus has your situation in His hands, and the answer to any problem you may be going through right now.

After a long wait, finally I was called to go into the exam room to wait for the doctor. I waited about an hour and a half, as usual is the case with this doctor. There is no regular schedule as to how soon patients will see him, because he is a companionate man and wants to ensure each patient he sees is taken care of. So it could be an hour, an hour and a half, or more. There was a time when I waited for more than two hours for him.

Finally the doctor came in, and he seemed to be a little bit different, maybe bewildered? I had never seen him like this before. He asked me all kinds of questions about my health: Asked about my appetite, my weight. Asked me if I had any pain, dizziness, and so on. And he gave me a full examination and pressed on all my lymph nodes to see if there was any pain.

He asked me again about a medical procedure we had discussed in the past and had agreed not to do. He said, "Now in the past we talked about going in through your mouth to get a sample for biopsy from your lungs."

"Well," I said, "we talked about it, but I had decided I didn't want to do it." I chose rather to trust in the Lord, because there was a great amount of risk in this kind of procedure.

So he repeated some things again we had talked about in the past that seemed to be a little bit out of place. I knew something was up.

Finally he said to me, "Well, I don't know how to explain it, but something has happened. And nothing or very little has been written about it. It's kind of a rare thing."

I asked, "What happened?"

He said, "You had a *spontaneous regression*."

The instant I heard those words, I knew it was good news, but I asked, "What does that mean" He said, "Do you know the word *spontaneous*?"

I said, "Yes."

He replied, "Well, those things you had in your lungs have backed off. They are gone. The large nodules have become tiny, and all of the small nodules have disappeared. "I don't know how to explain that" he said. "It's kind of a rare thing."

I jumped up from my seat and yelled, "Lord Jesus, thank you! You're my healer!" I yelled very loud. Again "Lord Jesus, thank you." My joy was indescribable, an excitement I could not contain.

I yelled again, "Lord, you are my healer! To you belongs all glory, all honor, and all praise. Thank you Lord for healing me." I turned to the doctor. "The Lord has given me a miracle. Do you believe in Jesus, I asked?"

He wouldn't respond. But I kept praising God and thanking Him. You know, when we go through this kind of experience as I did, this pressure inside is building up, a force that's about to, as in my case, explode. And it did ignite the instant I heard those words, *spontaneous regression*.

And he explained further, "It's a good thing what happened to you."

I knew that because I had this witness deep inside of me before he even explained anything else about this spontaneous regression. But this thing that came out of me, this excitement out of jubilation, it's a feeling I had never felt before.

And what also happened in that moment when I heard those words from the doctor (*spontaneous regression*), I had this experience. When I jumped up from my seat in utter joy, I felt as though I came out from under something, like a cover of some sort had opened up, that was above me. I don't know what it was, but I could see the light better.

Things were brighter around me. It felt like I was buried under something and I had come out of it, like a grave. I don't know how to describe it better, because I never before had an experience like that in my life. Later, I thought about all this again, what had happened at that moment, and I had concluded as before, when I could not explain something during the course of this journey, that there is mystery that surrounds our being that only God knows.

The doctor also said, "The guys may want to talk to you about it."

I asked, "Who are they?"

"The people who do the interviews for research here at the Indiana University Medical Center. They would want to know how this happened."

Nothing, according to the doctor, or very little has been written about this kind of an occurrence, and that's because it's a miracle. For many people, this miracle from the Lord may be an unexplainable event, but to a person of faith in Jesus, it is the *work* of the Living God. And I know, the Lord is the One who healed me, and had delivered me from such a terrible illness.

As I finished talking to the doctor, he told me that the nurse would come in to set me up for the next appointment because he said he would like to continue seeing me, and he wanted the next visit to be in two months. We talked a bit more, I thanked him, and I asked him again if he believed in Jesus, and he said, "Greg those are two different things (meaning religion and medicine). I am a doctor here, and I need to find out what happened." And though he didn't respond openly, he did give me an indication that he did believe.

I know deep in my heart that this miracle was a witness to him as well, so he may know that Jesus is Lord of all, and the healer even of the most terrible illness.

As the doctor went out, within a few minutes the nurse came in, and she was all smiles and happy. She said, "Greg, congratulations. That's awesome. Right before the doctor came in to see you, he called me into his office, and he showed me the CT scan images, the new ones and the ones from the month of February. He couldn't believe what he was seeing, how these nodules have moved out of your lungs. He was in utter amazement, He couldn't believe it."

I asked her, "Do you believe in Jesus?"

She said, "Yes, I do believe in Jesus."

Praise God. You see, this miracle touched the hearts of people—nurses and doctors who most likely had talked about it among themselves. Even if people don't believe right away, it causes them to think about it and to search for answers. And by the grace of God, as the Holy Spirit works in their hearts, some of them perhaps may come to believe in the Lord Jesus, as the Son of the Living God. I pray that this miracle will continue to touch the hearts of many people all over the country and around the world through this book for the glory of the Lord, who alone deserves all the praise.

After I finished my conversation with the nurse, I left the doctor's office feeling so happy and excited. It felt like I wasn't walking on the floor from joy. It seemed like I was in some kind of space between the heavens and the floor as I walked out to go pick up my car.

That side of the Medical Center where the cancer patients enter, is valet parking and so after I paid, I was waiting outside for my car to arrive, being overwhelmed with everything that had happened. This awesome miracle was filling my being. I called my family and told them about this miracle. They couldn't believe what had happened.

As I was waiting there for my car, I noticed, one by one, people were taking off.

If you are waiting on that side of this big complex to get your car, and you see one person waiting, you can be sure that person has some kind of a cancer and had come there to visit a doctor. If you saw two people, one has cancer, and the other would be there for support or to drive. Those are the people who come to the Simon Cancer Center clinics at the Indiana University Medical Center, which provide support and treatment for patients of all different kinds of cancer.

But as I was waiting for my car, I noticed again that everybody was gone except one person. There was this young woman standing a few feet away to my left side that I didn't notice before because I was so excited still from the awesome news of my healing.

So I turned and said, "Hi, I'm Greg. What's your name?"

She said, "I'm Mary (not the real name)."

"Oh," I said, "Why are you here?"

"I have stage four breast cancer, and I came to have some tests done today" she said.

She was there for the same purpose I was. My heart broke because she was a young woman with a young child, as she told me later.

One thing you learn when going through this kind of experience like I went through, is that the Lord fills your heart with compassion for what other people may be suffering because of an illness or for another difficult situation in their life. And my heart bled when I heard her say that she had one young child. Instantly I thought about how terrible she may feel with thoughts that may go through her mind like, would the child remember her? Who would raise up the child she loved if she were gone? Those are devastating thoughts for a young mother or father. My heart bled for her.

I told her that I had just come out of the doctor's office, and I had been delivered from cancer. "Jesus healed me," I told her. Then I asked her. "Do you believe in Jesus?"

And she smile and said, "Yes, I believe."

That made me feel good because she had hope. I don't know how strong her faith was, but I felt she was on a good path. Nevertheless, somehow I felt in my heart the pain that was in her heart. Soon my car showed up from the corner and I told her I would be praying for her and encouraged her to have hope in the Lord, she thanked me. I don't know any more about this young woman. And I pray with all my heart that she is okay and the hope and peace from the Lord be with her.

As I was driving toward Fort Wayne, I could not describe the joy that was in my heart. Praises to the Lord flowed out of my heart, along with thanksgiving, for the miracle He had given me. There was indescribable joy for this deliverance and my healing He had given me.

You see, when you go through the pain and the agony an incurable illness can bring, it feels like you're in front of a firing squad. And all of a sudden, somebody shows up and delivers you from there, and you are given a second chance in life.

This feeling of being delivered or freed from such a burden, is difficult to express. It filled me with joy, gratitude, thanksgiving and praise for the Lord, because He is the one who removed me from being in front of the firing squad. And as I was driving, this unending flow of praise and thanksgiving for the Lord continued to come out of my heart. I was singing hymns of praise to Him for nearly two and a half hours.

And this experience I had the moment I heard the good news of my healing, that somehow I had come out of some kind of a grave, kept coming back in my mind. It was overwhelming.

I continue to worry about people who suffer from the same affliction as I did. I wonder, *what do those who don't know the Lord, what do they go through? People who don't have faith in Him and the hope that comes from Him, the hope that brings life? How do they handle the pain and the despair that comes from going through such an experience?* Difficult questions to answer.

As I arrived home, everybody was waiting for me, and they were all very happy. They were happy and anxious to hear more of what had happened, because the pressure that was upon me to a certain degree, was also upon them. They were worrying about me, and they all experienced the joy of my deliverance and healing that I had received. All I can say is, thank you Lord Jesus for the joy that was in our home that night.

And I would like to encourage you again at this time. If you have been recently diagnosed with an illness like mine, allow me to say, out of concern, knowing the pain you may be experiencing, don't try to go through this without the

Lord Jesus on your side, you will have a very difficult time. You need the Lord Jesus. He is the only one who can give you hope and peace in your heart. Only He can help you overcome hopelessness. And if you don't know Him right now, it's never too late to get to know Him.

I found that, from the time I was diagnosed with this illness and through all the process, visits to doctors and going through the various tests, and so on, it is an extremely difficult time. You need Jesus for an additional reason: To help you overcome the attacks of the enemy who will come at times when you will be most vulnerable, and bring you all kinds of negative thoughts and condemnation for only one purpose: to destroy you.

If you are reading this page and you don't know the Lord Jesus in a personal way right now, you should seriously consider surrendering yourself to Him because you don't know what may happen to you even at the very next moment, as no one does. At the beginning of this book, I wrote that we're all temporary in this life. We don't know when we may pass on, and things do happen to our bodies that we don't foresee. Our bodies break down because again, they are temporary. No matter how much we try to keep in good shape, eat the right things, or have a positive attitude, etc. bad things health wise still may happen. Certain organs that are vital in our body can break down. And we don't know when this can happen. Like in my case, I had cancer in my left kidney, but I never had any signs to warn me about it, such as any sort of discomfort, pain, and so on, anything to indicate something was wrong.

The same may happen to you. That's why it's important that you know the Lord Jesus, the Son of God. And again, no one knows what may happen to us during the next minute, tonight in our sleep, or while we drive to go somewhere. We may have an accident and die instantly. Very often I hear about young people who have had severe illnesses such a heart problem or a stroke.

Think about this simple but very important question: Where do you think you may go if you died without knowing the Lord Jesus? Understand, your life will not end the instant you pass on. Instead the real life that never ends begins at that moment. In the new life, there is no middle area, but rather two places, very real and very different from each other: Heaven and hell.

Scripture teaches us that, only if we *believe* in Jesus that He is the Son of the Living God, we will have eternal life in the Kingdome of heaven. Here is the truth about this subject we find in Scripture: "He that believeth on the Son hath everlasting life: and he that believeth not the Son shall not see life; but the wrath of God abideth on him" (John 3:36). The wrath of God leads to hell.

We cannot go through this life rejecting God through unbelief, or by leading a lukewarm "Christian" life and expect Him to receive us in His heavenly kingdom after we pass on from here. If we don't know Him in this life, God will not know us either in the other life. The Lord Jesus spoke about this during His earthly ministry,

> "Not everyone that saith unto me, Lord, Lord, shall enter into the kingdom of heaven; but he that doeth the will of my Father which is in heaven. Many will say to me in that day, Lord, Lord, have we

> not prophesied in thy name? And in thy name have cast out devils? And in thy name done many wonderful works? And then will I profess unto them, I never knew you: depart from me, ye that work iniquity" (Matt. 7:21–23).

That's why is so important to believe in Jesus and to know Him in a *personal* way. He knows more than you and I do, how important it is to know Him, because He knows also better than you and I about the horrific suffering that exists in hell, and because of His love for us, He wants us to join Him forever in His kingdom.

Even now at this very moment, He is waiting for you to open your heart to Him, and He is saying the same to everyone on this planet, "Behold, I stand at the door and knock. If any man hear my voice and open, I will sup with him and he with me" (Rev. 20:3). Those are His words.

He is waiting for you to open the door of your heart. Only you can open that door. Your parents cannot do it for you, nor can your friends, or your priest or pastor. Only you can open your heart to the Lord Jesus.

Would you pray this simple prayer: "Father, I admit I am a sinner and I repent of my sins, forgive me in the *name* of your Holy Son Jesus. Lord, thank you for suffering and for dying on the Cross for me. I believe that you are the Son of God. Please come into my life and into my heart, and fill me with your presence. Amen."

Repenting, is admitting that we have sinned. It is the *beginning* and the *foundation* of a new life in Christ.

I have learned from over thirty eight years studying His Word, that the Lord Jesus is *very simple* and requires no higher or any special education to know Him. He does not require that you know someone "else" in order to know Him. He doesn't expects you to recite the prayer of another man, because He wants to hear *simple words from your own heart.* If those words you spoke when you prayed earlier came from your heart, He has heard you and He will come in your life, and He will change you forever. Begin with studying the Bible with zeal if possible every day, and allow time for prayer. As you continue seeking Him through His Word, God will become increasingly more real to you, and a new *relationship* will be begin to rise between God and yourself.

Prayer allows us to communicate with our heavenly Father, and provides us with the opportunity to express our thanksgiving which He delights hearing from us, for all the things we enjoy in this life, that we often take for granted. Through prayer, we bring our needs, and the needs of people around us before Him. Prayer *wrapped up* in faith brings miracles.

By knowing the Lord, you will be able also to help someone such as a relative, or a friend by giving them *true* hope. Someone who may be going through a very difficult challenge in his life right now, by telling him/her about the *real* hope that exists *only* through the Lord Jesus.

In his first epistle, John wrote, "And we know that the Son of God is come, and hath given us an understanding, that we may know Him that is true, and we are in Him that is true, even in His Son Jesus Christ. This is the *true* God, and *eternal* life" (1 John 5:20).

Jesus is the true God and the eternal life, and apart from Him, there is no one else you and I can call upon for help during times of affliction, or to be saved from the eternal damnation, because Jesus is the only way to the kingdom of heaven according to the gospel of John, where Jesus Himself said, "... No man comes to the Father but by Me" (John 14:6).

My miracle healing was manifested during that day on April 25, 2016, through the CT scans and the blood tests, but this miracle *came* because I trusted in the Way that leads to God, and that is Jesus Christ. Miracles come ONLY from Him, because He is God.

Only God can bring miracles of healing, resurrect someone from the dead, deliver an addict, take away depression, and bring healing to a relationship, and so on.

In the gospel of Matthew, we read about what happens when we ask in faith, "And all things whatsoever you ask in prayer, *believing* you *will* receive" (Matthew 21:22). You noticed, it didn't say *maybe* you will receive. No, it said you *will* receive. And that's a promise from the Almighty God. And you know what? Everything He promises in His Word, is absolutely true. And through personal experience, I also testify that it is absolutely true.

In Psalm 91:15, we read, "He (the believer) shall call upon me and I will answer him. I will be with him in trouble..." Can you imagine? God promises to be with us when we call upon Him when we are in trouble. How comforting and reassuring can this be when we are hurting? Awesome promise.

It was through faith in Jesus again that I was delivered from cancer, just as Peter and John through faith in the Lord

Jesus, one day healed this man who was born impotent from his mother womb. Peter told the Jews, who were looking at them in amazement as though this miracle had occurred because of their own personal power or goodness, "And His name, through faith in His name, has made this man strong…" (Acts 3:16). This man received strength even though he had never walked. Atrophy was all over him, but then in an instant, God renewed his body and gave this man strength and a new life. A miracle through faith.

And that's how I received my healing, through faith in the name of Jesus because there is power in the name of Jesus. And when we abide in Him by studying His Word, believe in Him and obey Him, deliverance, healings and salvation will flow from Him, just as He had promised in His Word, "If ye abide in me, and my words abide in you, ye shall ask what ye will, and it shall be done unto you" (John 15:7).

The day after I received the good news of my healing on April 25, I began testifying to people about the miracle the Lord had granted me. A few days later, I had the opportunity to witness to a group of women at a Bible study. I told them about this miracle of healing, and they rejoiced and praised the Lord. Nearly everywhere I went the Lord provided an opportunity to testify to someone-and He still does. Every person I met, if I had a chance, I would tell them about my healing, and of course, I continue to do that as the Lord provides.

Out of my heart continues to flow thanksgiving and praise for the Lord my healer, and after so many months later, I cannot forget this awesome miracle, and my deliverance from the grip of this vicious and feared illness. Thank God.

Two months later, on June 23, 2016, I went back for another checkup. I again had the CT scans and blood tests, and in the afternoon I met with the doctor. The tests showed that my lungs showed to be the same as on that day April 25th, 2016, as the doctor had described them. And so it was confirmed again that my healing was complete.

I went back on September 22 and December 16 of 2016, and both times, the CT scans showed exactly the same thing, that my lungs were clear. My next appointment then was moved from the two-month interval to three months since the doctor saw the condition of my lungs to be even better than the way they were on that day, April 25, 2016.

Another Witness for His Glory

My next appointment was set for March 16, 2017. I went back to Indianapolis on that day and followed the routine as before: CT scans in the morning and blood tests in the afternoon. Afterward I met with the doctor. But this time, something different happened.

As I was driving to Indianapolis on that morning, March 16, 2017, I was praying, as I did the other times during the two and a half hours of driving. At one point I said, "Lord, what is it that you want me to do today for you? Is there someone you want me to witness today?" Soon I was beginning to get into heavy traffic, and I forgot all about what I had asked Him. But He didn't as I found out later.

As soon as I arrived that morning, I went through the same routine: Registration, CT scans, blood tests, and then to the lounge near the doctor's office for the long wait.

After about an hour and half of waiting, finally they called me to go into the exam room to wait for the doctor. Shortly after I settled in, two men walked in. This never happened before. Both wore white jackets. One took the lead and introduced himself, and I believe he said he was doing his residency. The other man—I wasn't clear what he was doing—was standing a few feet behind, observing. The first man opened a folder and began reading what appeared to be my medical records because he would ask me questions about it.

Often he would say, "Wow! Wow! What happened?"

And finally I said to him, "The Lord healed me."

He looked at me a little puzzled and turned back to reading again. And he kept going, "Wow." It seemed that he had a little difficulty with what he was reading.

Finally he asked me to get onto the examination table, and he gave me a thorough physical examination. He asked if I had any pain, what my appetite was like, my weight, and so on. And he pressed at various parts of my body to see if there was any pain and particularly at my lymph node points. He wanted to see if I had strength in my hands and feet, and he kept writing notes. He seemed very perplexed. I guess he might have had a little difficult time with the fact that I was healed.

At one point as he was writing, words just came out from inside of me and I said to them both: "Now, what is it that you both need to have as new doctors in order to service your patients in the best possible way, so other doctors can see what you do, how well you figure out each patient's condition, and wonder how you do it? As we know every patient is different."

Both looked at me, waiting to hear what I would say next.

I said to them, "You need *discernment* from the living God so you will know what the case may be with each patient, and how to go about treating each one properly."

Both shook their heads in agreement.

I said next, "But the only way to obtain this special gift is through the Lord Jesus. When you believe in Him and obey Him, He will give you that discernment you will need to be the best in your profession."

When I finished talking, the man who did the examination smiled and said, "Well, I'm a Muslim."

I thought, *"Thank you, Lord! You* are awesome."

Then I said to him, "That's okay. You need the Lord Jesus because He is the only way that leads to heaven, and apart from Him, no one can go to heaven."

He smiled, thanked me and turned to leave. The other man was listening very attentively when I spoke, gave me a *firm* handshake. I found out later, from my doctor when he came in to see me that this other young doctor was from Brazil and was there for training. Most likely a Christian.

You see, I had forgotten what I had asked the Lord in the morning about witnessing for Him, but you see, God didn't forget.

In the first example where I witnessed to that man at the pulmonologist's office, God's plan was different than my plan. I went there because I had this cough and I was very concerned about it. At that time I was beginning the journey with this illness, and I didn't know yet that I had cancer in me. I was worrying about this cough and I had no intention to witness to anyone, but God thought differently.

The second time, at Indiana University Medical Center, my witnessing to these men was during a time of rejoicing, because I had already experienced the miracle of my healing. The point is: The Lord can use us in good and bad times, but only when we're *willing* to stand up and tell others about Him, so that somebody else may hear the good news of the gospel, and hopefully, come to believe in the Lord Jesus who is the *Way* that leads to heaven.

In the gospel of Luke, we find these words that the Lord Jesus spoke, "Likewise, I say unto you, there is joy in the presence of the angels of God over one sinner that repenteth" (Luke 15:10). And why do the angels in heaven rejoice? Because repentance and faith will save a soul from going to hell. It is God's will no one to be lost, but unfortunately, not everyone will submit to the Son of God.

Whether somebody is from another faith and the Lord Jesus is not his God, or another who's been attending Church all his life but does not know the Lord, or yet someone who may be an agnostic, God has set a time for them to hear the message of the gospel, and believers in Christ must be *ready* and *willing* to give that testimony.

In order to have this opportunity from the Lord, we need to know the Word of God and be able to give the message of the gospel with courage, and with conviction, just as Peter had the godly courage to tell the people of Jerusalem who had gathered around him, "His is the only name, that we may be saved. There is *no other name* that we may call upon to be saved in Heaven or on Earth" (Acts 4:12).

Peter was not afraid to tell his fellow Jews about the truth, that Jesus was (and still is) the ONLY way for his countrymen to be saved, and his countrymen were people who were so absorbed in the Law of Moses. He was not afraid of insulting anyone with the truth or being imprisoned by the chief priests and the rulers, and that's because he knew it was more important for his people to hear the message of salvation, than his personal safety. And like Peter, all who believe in the Lord, must be ready and willing to do the same as he did: To witness for the Lord.

Going back to the exam room, shortly after the men left, the doctor came in and explained the results of the CT scan and the blood tests I had taken that morning. And he confirmed again my healing, saying my lungs were clear. I rejoiced in what I heard once again and praised the living God, my Lord, my healer and my Savior, Jesus.

And I pray with all my heart that this book has touched your life so that you will seek Jesus and believe in Him, and make Him Lord of your life. And remember: If you seek Him, you will find Him, just as King David advised his son Solomon before he died. And if you decide to seek Him, you will find Him also.

Also in Matthew 7:7 we read, "Seek and it shall be given you. Ask and you shall find. Knock and it will be opened unto you." These are God's promises and they are true. If you seek Him and ask to know Him, He will come in your life. Just like His promise that was written by the apostle John in the book of Revelation, "Behold, I stand at the door, and knock: if any man hear my voice, and open the door, I will come in to him, and will sup with him, and he with me" (Revelation 3:20).

Do you suppose He meant it when He said He would come and "sup with you?" He absolutely did! If you open the door of your heart, and invite Him to come in, Jesus will come and will fill you with His presence, because He is alive and He hears you. And that would be the most important—the most critical, decision you will ever make: To choose to open your heart to receive Him as the Lord and Savior of your life.

I pray you will make that decision, and if you do, not only He will come in your life, but He will also help you by delivering you from whatever challenge you may be facing in your life right now, just as He delivered me from the grip of this terrible illness.

In Closing

Not only did the Lord Jesus heal me, He also gave me hope and peace to go through the difficult times. But as I mentioned earlier, if you ask in prayer and don't receive an answer immediately, continue to have hope in Him. Know that He heard you. He just wants you to trust in Him and learn to depend upon Him. Continue with passion studying His Word and with prayer, and God will bring you a miracle.

He will provide a way for you where there appears to be no way out from this difficult situation you may be facing right now, or this big mountain that stands in front of you that seems impossible to go through or move it out of the way. But God is able to provide a *new way* for you. Be persistent in waiting on Jesus. He is faithful. Continue to hope in Him, and He will bring the miracle you are waiting, because He *loves* you.

Don't give up!

Don't Give Up!

Are you facing an impossible situation right now? Remember, there is hope, and it is found in the Lord Jesus. What may appear to be an impossible situation to you and to those around you, with Him everything is possible.

In the gospel of Matthew we read where the Lord told His disciples, "With God all things are possible" (Matthew 19:26). In Luke 1:36, we read the angel Gabriel told Mary that her cousin Elizabeth, the one who was "called barren," had conceived in her old age. Humanly speaking, it would have been impossible for a ninety-year-old woman to have a child, but Gabriel said, "For with God nothing shall be impossible" (Luke 1:37).

Indeed nothing is impossible with God, and to fully understand that, all we have to do is look around us and see the complexity, harmony, and beauty of His creation. Look at the earth and the heavens above with the billions of stars. He made everything.

In Isaiah 45:12, we read where God said, "I have made the earth, and created man upon it: I, even my hands, have stretched out the heavens, and all their host have I commanded." How awesome and mind-boggling that is: The power of God Almighty?

TER

re read about the miracle
n water. One night after
they were in a boat trying
nd the strong wind, when
n the waves. Peter, known
Lord if it be you, bid me
tthew 14:28).

Jesus said to him, "Come" and Peter immediately got off the boat and began walking on the water because he had faith in Jesus, who had called him to come to Him. But shortly thereafter, as we read in the Bible, Peter saw how strong the wind was, and he *realized* he was walking on the waves, a very scary scenario and an impossible situation, like we often find ourselves in this life.

When Peter became aware of these extraordinary circumstances that had surrounded him, the adverse weather, and the very fact he was on the water, fear filled his mind, and he began to sink. But why did that happen? Where was his faith? Well, this sudden disruption of his faith took place because he ceased to focus on Jesus from where his faith was emanating, but instead he *paid attention* to the impossible situation, the bad circumstances around him with his own limited human ability. He failed to trust in the Almighty God.

Like Peter, many of us also sink under the weight of the adverse, impossible circumstances that surround us, and that happens when we too take our eyes off from Jesus. When we don't trust in Him.

Peter was in the midst of a miracle because of his faith that had lasted for a short time, but the instant he took his eyes off from Jesus, immediately fear *entered* in him as we read, "But when he saw the wind boisterous, he was afraid; and beginning to sink, he cried, saying, Lord, save me" (Matthew 14:30).

Maybe you may be going through an impossible situation, feeling hopeless, disappointed, or depressed because your career was disrupted unexpectedly. Perhaps there is a business that you have put in everything you had, but is not doing well, or you may have received bad news from the doctor about your health. Maybe you have been trying hard to keep away from an addiction that seems to be ruining your life, or maybe you don't have the money to pay the mortgage.

The list of challenges that can happen to any of us can be really long, but what I want to tell you is this: The Lord Jesus does care for you. He is the One who holds everything we see, and the things we don't see, in His own hands. No matter what your situation is that you are going through, don't give up! He is right there next to you, and He can help you. Just like Peter, we too can walk on the water, meaning, we also can overcome the mountains of big problems or the impossible hurdles that confront us, if we only focus on Jesus as Peter did at the very beginning of his short lived miracle, and place our hope, and believe in Him, everything will be fine.

God told the prophet Jeremiah, "Behold, I am the Lord, the God of all flesh: is there anything too hard for me?" (Jer. 32:26–27). You see, nothing is too hard or too difficult for Him because He is God, and because of Him, we can make it.

But remember, earlier what we talked about: That in order for miracles to happen, we must have faith in God. *Believe* He is who He says He is, and believe also that He is *able* to reward or provide for those who have faith in Him. But we need to remember also, "Without faith it is impossible to please Him" (Heb. 11:6).

Having a strong faith it means that you believe you have *already* received what you've asked before you even have it. That's the faith that can bring miracles. That is, to have an *expectation* for the things you don't *yet see* but have asked for in prayer. And that's what we read in the gospel of Mark, "Therefore I say unto you, what things soever ye desire, when ye pray, *believe* that ye *receive* them, and ye shall have them" (Mark 11:24).

Don't give up. God knows everything about you. The Bible tells us, "Even the very hair of our head are all numbered" (Luke 12:7). Well, if He knows about the number of your hair on your head, He certainly knows also about the mountain like challenge you are facing right now.

When we stop and consider the multitude of miracles Jesus did for the people around Him while He walked on this earth, then we will realize His power and wisdom are without end. And what He did then, He is able to do the same today for us, because He is the same today as He was yesterday.

Also, often we forget who we are. We are His children, and precious to Him, because with His own blood He has purchased us. We are the sons and daughters of the Almighty God through faith in His Son as we read, "For ye are all the *children* of God by *faith* in Christ Jesus" (Galatians 3:26).

But we forget His words, and we allow the enemy to put us in a box, where all we think is how difficult or big our problems are. We forget that the Lord Jesus when He was gloriously resurrected from the dead, He has triumphed over the enemy, and through Him, we can be victorious also by dwelling in Him through His Living Word. When we do that, it is then that our faith will rise to a new higher level, where we begin to *expect* miracles.

The Blind Man

Now let's read about an impossible situation, a story we read in Scripture that became possible.

A man was born blind, but by the grace of God one day, he met Jesus, who touched him, and in an instant, he was able to see. We read about this incredible miracle in the gospel of John 9:1, 6–7 where it says,

> "And as Jesus passed by, he saw a man which was blind from his birth; when he had thus spoken, he spat on the ground, and made clay of the spittle, and he anointed the eyes of the blind man with the clay; and said unto him, go, wash in the pool of Siloam (which is by interpretation, sent). He went his way therefore, and washed, and came seeing."

In an instant, God healed this man. Whatever was wrong with his eyes, God fixed it and he was able to see for the first time in his life. Now, do you think that the Lord is able to fix your problem? Yes, He can. It doesn't matter how complex your situation may be, God can help you as well.

The enemy always places all kinds of doubt in us to prevent us from believing that God can help us, like you may say, "Well, you don't understand. My situation is different. It is hereditary ..." or "My illness is this or this other kind" and so on. No, it doesn't matter what type of problem you are facing. You need to trust in the Lord and always remember what He said in Jeremiah 32:27, "... Is there anything too hard for me?" Trust in Him, and any obstacle that stands before you, He can remove it.

More Miracles

In the gospel of John, we read how Jesus raised His friend, Lazarus, who had been dead for four days. You know that the climate in the area where this miracle took place is known to be hot, and after four days, as we learn in Scripture, the body was in a state of decomposition, but for the Lord, "Nothing shall be impossible" (Luke 1:37).

We read about this in the Gospel of John where Jesus said, "Take ye away the stone. Martha, the sister of him that was dead, saith unto him, Lord, by this time he stinketh: for he hath been dead four days. Jesus saith unto her, said I not unto thee, that, if thou wouldest believe, thou shouldest see the glory of God? Then they took away the stone from the place where the dead was laid. And Jesus lifted up his eyes, and said, Father, I thank thee that thou hast heard me.

And I knew that thou hearest me always: but because of the people which stand by I said it, that they may believe that thou hast sent me. And when he thus had spoken, he cried with a loud voice, Lazarus, come forth. And he that was dead came forth..." (John 11:39-44).

Now, humanly speaking, how can something like that happened? In the mind of the unbelieving world, that's not possible. People may say how in the world all the decomposed, complex human organs were revitalized and brought back to life in an instant, so that the dead man could stand up and walk? Not possible! Well, yes, it is possible, and it's called a miracle!

Now do you think the Lord Jesus can help you with your difficult situation?

One day, Jesus was teaching to a large group of people until late, and instead of sending them away hungry, He fed five thousand men, plus women and children, with just five loaves and two fish. And after everybody was filled, they had twelve baskets of bread left over. We read about this miracle in Mark 6:41–44,

> "And when he had taken the five loaves and the two fishes, he looked up to heaven, and blessed, and brake the loaves, and gave them to his disciples to set before them; and the two fishes divided He among them all. And they did all eat, and were filled. And they took up twelve baskets full of the fragments, and of the fishes. And they that did eat of the loaves were about five thousand men."

This miracle shows us that God is really awesome. From out of *nothing,* He provided a physical substance, bread. In other words, the things that could not be *seen,* became something that could be touched and be seen. They became real. And because He is the same today as He was yesterday, He can provide something you need out of nothing as well, and that again, it's called a miracle!

Even when everything points toward a hopeless situation, God is able to change that. And just as with the bread and fish that kept coming out of nowhere, likewise, the problems that are surrounding us miraculously will disappear like the nodules that used to be in my lungs miraculously vanished.

Don't give up! Be patient and wait upon the Lord with faith and expectation, and know your deliverance is near. In Lamentations 3:25–26, we read, "The Lord is good unto them that wait for him, and to the soul that seeketh Him. It is good that a man should both hope and quietly wait for the salvation of the Lord."

To wait upon the Lord is to have faith in Him, to be patient knowing He has heard your prayer, and believe that He will answer you at the right time. Don't rush into conclusions that are based on thoughts the enemy brings in your mind, thoughts of hopelessness and unbelief. But stay firm, trusting and hoping in the Lord, and He will bless you as He had promised in Jeremiah 17:7, "Blessed is the man that trusts in the Lord, whose hope the Lord is." God is faithful.

If you are facing an impossible challenge right now, I know you are worrying. Let Jesus take the burden of worrying from off your shoulders. He doesn't want to see you suffer, and He is saying to you even right now, "Come unto me, all ye that labor and are heavy laden, and I will give you rest. Take my yoke upon you, and learn of me; for I am meek and lowly in heart: and ye shall find rest unto your souls. For my yoke is easy, and my burden is light" (Matthew 11:28–30).

That's right, the Lord wants to take that burden off from you, Believe in Him and He will deliver you from whatever challenge you are facing by making the impossible possible for you, because He loves you.

Scripture reveals to us that Jesus came so that we may have an abundant life, as we read, "The thief cometh not, but for to steal, and to kill, and to destroy: I Am come that they might have life, and that they might have it more abundantly" (John 10:10). Can you say amen to that?

That is another awesome promise we must never forget. Our heavenly Father promised us not just an ordinary life but an abundant life. A life filled with hope, peace, and joy by knowing that, even though there are challenges in this life, He is by our side to help us overcome every difficult situation that may come against us. And that, dear friend, is what brings the peace in our heart that's from above, as the Word of God confirms in Philippians 4:7 where it says, "And the peace of God, which passeth all understanding, shall keep your hearts and minds through Christ Jesus."

Don't give up. There are bright and shiny days just ahead for you. Have faith in the Lord Jesus, and He will bring a miracle in your life, just as He did for me.

The Living Word of God

The following verses from the Word of God gave me hope and peace in my heart and strength to continue during the difficult times after I was diagnosed with kidney cancer. These were the Bible verses I memorized and spoke out loud daily to remind myself of the promises our heavenly Father has made to us. As I continued to study and meditate on His Word, my faith increased, and I began to *expect* to receive from Him, and the Lord responded by giving me this miracle. It was *through His Word* that I was healed from the metastatic kidney cancer.

If you have faith in the Lord Jesus and trust in His Word, you also will see a miracle and be delivered from whatever challenge you are facing right now, because He is able to provide a *new way* for you even when, humanly speaking, there may be no way out in sight regarding your situation of failing health issues, an addiction, family problems, job-related issues, etc. Whatever it may be, the Almighty God can help you if you only believe in His Holy Son Jesus in whose hands the Father has delivered everything that is in heaven and on earth as it is written in Matthew 28:18.

About the Word

Believe that the words we find in the Bible are the Words spoken by the Almighty God to His holy prophets of old and later, to the apostles of the Lord Jesus Christ, who wrote them on paper that we may know Him, His will, and His promises to us.

In 2 Timothy 3:16, the apostle Paul wrote, “All scripture is given by inspiration of God, and is profitable for doctrine, for reproof, for correction, for instruction in righteousness.” And in 2 Peter 1:22, it says, “For the prophecy came not in old time by the will of man: but holy men of God spake as they were moved by the Holy Ghost.”

When we ask, the Lord answers. Be assured that when you pray, the Lord hears you, and He will answer you at the right time, which will be the best time for your own sake, and for the glory of His name. The Scripture verses below testify of the Lord’s faithfulness:

- Psalm 34:15 reads, “The eyes of the Lord are upon the righteous, and his ears are open unto their cry.”
- Matthew 7:7 says, “Ask, and it shall be given you...”
- Psalm 91:15 states, “He shall call upon me, and I will *answer* him: I will be with him in trouble; I will deliver him, and honor him.”
- Psalm 118:5 reads, “I called upon the Lord in distress: the Lord answered me, and set me in a large place.”

- 1 John 3:22 says, "And whatsoever we ask, we *receive* of him, because we keep his commandments, and do those things that are pleasing in his sight."
- John 15:7 states, "If ye abide in me, and my words abide in you, ye shall *ask what ye will*, and it shall be done unto you."

Ask in His Name

But when you ask in prayer for God to intervene in your life and deliver you from a difficult situation or to provide something that is necessary for you to have, ask in the *name* of Jesus because the Father has given His Son, "All authority in heaven and on earth", as we wrote in the previews pages also:

- John 14:6 reads, "Jesus saith unto him, I am the way, the truth, and the life: no man cometh unto the Father, but by me."
- John 16:24 says, "Hitherto have ye asked nothing in my name: ask, and ye shall receive, that your joy may be full."
- John 14:13–14 states, "And whatsoever ye shall ask in my name, that will I do, that the Father may be glorified in the Son. If ye shall ask any thing in my name, I will do it."

About Faith

After the apostles Peter and John healed the man who was born impotent, he said to the Jews who had gathered around them in wonder as though they had done that miracle through their own power, but Peter said, "And his name through faith in His name hath made this man strong, whom ye see and know: yea, the faith which is by him hath given him this perfect soundness in the presence of you all" (Acts 3:16).

The apostle Paul wrote, "But without faith it is impossible to please Him: for he that cometh to God must believe that He is, and that He is a rewarder of them that diligently seek Him" (Hebrews 11:6).

About Hope

True hope is life, and the truth is that we cannot find true hope in anything or in anyone in this world. There is no hope to receive help from our fellow men when we go through very difficult times in our lives. True hope comes only from above, from the Almighty God, and this hope from Him defies our understanding. Without this hope from above, when the most challenging times come, hopelessness will flood a man's heart, and death will soon follow.

Here is what Scripture is teaching about hoping in God:

- 1 Timothy 1:1 reads, "Paul, an apostle of Jesus Christ by the commandment of God our Savior, and Lord Jesus Christ, *who is our hope*."
- Romans 8:28 says, "And we know that all things work together for good to them that love God, to them who are the called according to his purpose."
- Mark 5:36 states, "As soon as Jesus heard the word that was spoken, he saith unto the ruler of the synagogue, be not afraid only believe."
- Isaiah 50:9 reads, "Behold, the Lord God will help me; who is he that shall condemn me? Lo, they all shall wax old as a garment; the moth shall eat them up."
- Luke 1:50 says, "And his mercy is on them that fear Him from generation to generation."

About Peace

The only peace that is lasting and truly able to bring comfort to a man's heart from fear comes from above, from our heavenly Father and through faith in our Lord Jesus Christ, as we read in the following verses:

- Ephesians 2:14 reads, "*For He is our peace*, who hath made both one, and hath broken down the middle wall of partition between us."

- Philippians 4:7 says, "And the *peace* of God, which passeth all understanding, shall keep your hearts and minds through Christ Jesus."
- Psalm 34:4 states, "I sought the Lord, and he heard me, and delivered me from all my fears."
- Psalm 112:7 we read about the man who *fears* God, "He shall not be afraid of evil tidings: his heart is fixed, trusting in the Lord."

About Life

- Psalm 118:17 states, "I shall not die, but live, and declare the works of the Lord."
- Psalm 91:16 says, "With long life will I satisfy him, and shew him my salvation."
- Romans 8:6 reads, "For to be carnally minded is death; but to be spiritually minded is *life* and peace."

About Healing

- Isaiah 53:5 says, "But he was wounded for our transgressions, he was bruised for our iniquities: the chastisement of our peace was upon him; and with his stripes we are healed."
- 1 Peter 2:24 states, "Who his own self bare our sins in his own body on the tree that we, being dead to sins, should live unto righteousness: by whose stripes ye were healed."

About Protection

- Psalm 1:9–12 says, "Because thou hast made the Lord, which is my refuge, even the most High, thy habitation; There shall no evil befall thee, neither shall any plague come nigh thy dwelling. For he shall give his angels charge over thee, to keep thee in all thy ways. They shall bear thee up in their hands, lest thou dash thy foot against a stone."

About Strength

- Isaiah 41:10 says, "Fear thou not; for I am with thee: be not dismayed; for I am thy God: I will *strengthen* thee; yea, I will help thee; yea, I will uphold thee with the right hand of my righteousness."
- Isaiah 40:31 states, "But they that wait upon the Lord shall renew their *strength*; they shall mount up with wings as eagles; they shall run, and not be weary; and they shall walk, and not faint."

About Deliverance

- Psalm 34:7 states, "The angel of the Lord encampeth round about them that fear him, and *delivereth* them."
- Psalm 34:17 says, "The righteous cry, and the Lord heareth, and *delivereth* them out of all their troubles."
- Psalm 34:19 reads, "Many are the afflictions of the righteous: but the Lord delivereth him out of them all."

Source of Blessings

- Psalm 84:12 says, "O Lord of hosts, *blessed* is the man that trusteth in thee."
- Psalm 112:1 reads, "Praise ye the Lord. *Blessed* is the man that feareth the Lord that delighteth greatly in his commandments."
- Psalm 17:7–8 says, "*Blessed* is the man that trusteth in the Lord, and whose hope the Lord is. For he shall be as a tree planted by the waters, and that spreadeth out her roots by the river, and shall not see when heat cometh, but her leaf shall be green; and shall not be careful in the year of drought, neither shall cease from yielding fruit."

CPSIA information can be obtained
at www.ICGtesting.com
Printed in the USA
LVHW070214300623
751237LV00003B/81